Fritz Schriber

The Complete Carriage and Wagon Painter

A Concise Compendium of the Art of Painting Carriages, Wagons and...

Fritz Schriber

The Complete Carriage and Wagon Painter
A Concise Compendium of the Art of Painting Carriages, Wagons and...

ISBN/EAN: 9783337143480

Printed in Europe, USA, Canada, Australia, Japan

Cover: Foto ©Lupo / pixelio.de

More available books at **www.hansebooks.com**

THE COMPLETE CARRIAGE AND WAGON PAINTER.

A CONCISE COMPENDIUM OF THE ART OF PAINTING

CARRIAGES, WAGONS AND SLEIGHS,

EMBRACING FULL DIRECTIONS IN ALL THE VARIOUS BRANCHES, INCLUDING

Lettering, Scrolling, Ornamenting, Striping, Varnishing and Coloring,

WITH NUMEROUS RECIPES FOR MIXING COLORS.

ILLUSTRATED.

BY FRITZ SCHRIBER.

NEW YORK:
M. T. RICHARDSON CO., PUBLISHERS.
1895.

COPYRIGHTED BY
M. T. RICHARDSON
1883.

PREFACE.

In placing the manuscript of this book in the hands of the publisher, I was impressed with the belief that I had thoroughly carried out the original design, which was to write a full and comprehensive treatise on the methods employed by experienced workmen in painting a carriage, wagon, sleigh or railway car, and since the work of my pen has returned to me in printed form, I see no cause to change that belief or to erase one word therein.

The painting of vehicles, although differing in many respects, according to their quality or value, is virtually the same, and I have departed from the beaten track of writers in magazines, and chosen for my text *a wagon*, from the fact that the field was a larger one, and in describing how that vehicle could be painted, lettered, striped and ornamented. I could at the same time give all the information necessary for the painting of a first-class carriage or sleigh. My object, too, was to condense in one handbook not only the method of executing plain painting on vehicles, but to give all the instruction necessary for the practice of striping, lettering, scrolling, varnishing, polishing and many minor accomplishments, which would be out of place in a work on carriage painting alone.

THE AUTHOR.

CONTENTS.

Preface. - - - - - - - - - - - 5

CHAPTER I.
THE SHOP AND HOW IT SHOULD BE CONSTRUCTED.

The Furniture of the Paint and Varnish Rooms. Brushes, etc.—To "Bridle" a Brush—The Sash Tool—The Camels' Hair Brush, or "Blender"—The Badger Hair Brush—The Oval Brush—Cleaning-up Brush—Bench and Boxes for Colors—List of Colors Required in Wagon Painting, - - - - - 11

CHAPTER II.
MIXING COLORS.

Combining Pigments to Form Colors—Glazing—Putty, White, Quick. Black, etc., - - - - 19

CHAPTER III.
PRIMING.

Lead Color Method—The First Coat of Lead—Rough Stuffing the Panels—Leading the Gears—Rubbing Out Rough Stuff—Putting Final Foundation Coat on the Gears—Painting the Body—The Second Coat on the Body—Painting the Gears—The Rubbing Process, - - - - - - - - 25

CHAPTER IV.
THE PUTTY-KNIFE METHOD.

Another Way—The Wood-filling Method—Varnishing -Varnishing of Wagons and Sleighs—Sweating—Cleaning new Brushes, - - - - - - 38

CHAPTER V.

The Care of Materials—Failures in Varnishing—Troubles of the Painter—Specky Varnishes—Crawling of Paint or Varnish—Blistering—Cracking of Paint and Varnish—To Paint Canvas-top Sides—Glazing with Carmine, - - - - - - 45

CHAPTER VI.

Wagon Striping—The Striper's Kit of Tools—Striping Pencils—Zinc Palettes—Care of Pencils—Pencils for Ornamental Striping—Colors for Striping, - 50

CHAPTER VII.

Wagon Striping—Breaking Lines—A Pounce Bag—Gold Striping—Gilding Size—Applying Gold Leaf—Gold Striping, - - - - - - 56

CHAPTER VIII.

Colors Employed on Wagons—Painting a White Job - 68

CHAPTER IX.
WAGON LETTERING.

The Full Block, round and octagon—Half Block, round and octagon—Solid Block and Italic Letters—Outline Letters—Printers' Black Letter or German Text—Ornamental and Tuscan Full Block Letters—Three Styles of Letters used by the Abbot Downing Co., - - - - - - - 70

CHAPTER X.
WAGON LETTERING CONTINUED.

The Roman Letter—The Modern Old Style Letter—The New York Roman Letter—The New York Roman Italic Letter (Upper and Lower Case)—The Boston Roman. - - - - - - - - 80

CHAPTER XI.
LAYING OUT WORK.

Designing Half Block Letters—Using the Ellipse in Making Round Letters—The Alphabet in Gothic—Half Block Lower Case Letters—Making an Ellipse—Properly Balancing Letters and Figures,- 96

CONTENTS.

CHAPTER XII.
SHADING.

Single Shade Block Letters—Double Shade Blocked Letters—Shading Gold Letters—Shading Painted Letters—Tools used in Lettering—Illustrations of Various Methods of Shading. - - - - 104

CHAPTER XIII.
WAGON SCROLLING.

Making Circles and Curves—Making and Shading Scrolls—Materials and Tools used in Making and Shading Scrolls—Designing and Laying Out Scroll Patterns—Flat Scrolls. - - - - - 111

CHAPTER XIV.
STENCILING.

Making a Stencil—Brushes for Stencils. - - 121

SUPPLEMENT—CARRIAGE PAINTING AND VARNISHING.

CHAPTER I.
A GOOD FOUNDATION.

Putting on the First Coat—Chipping—The Second Coat—Puttying—Sand Papering—The Last Coat—Ready for Ground Color—Drying Dead—The Varnish Coats—The Finishing Coat—Rubbing. - 127

CHAPTER II.

Dusting and Cleaning Work—Puttying up Joints—Cleaning Gears. - - - - - - 137

CHAPTER III.

Painting Lumber Wagons—Striping—A Good Color—Ready to Varnish, - - - - - 142

CHAPTER IV.

Touching Up Repair Work, - - - - 145

CHAPTER V.

How to Paint a Cheap Job—Painting an Express Wagon—The Gear Coat—Paint for Body—Painting the Body. - - - - - - - - - 148

CHAPTER VI.

How to Revarnish a Carriage—Washing—Touching Up. - - - - - - - - - 152

CHAPTER VII.

Forms and Colors in the Painting of Vehicles—One Color for Wood and Another for Iron—Another View—All Parts should be of the Same Color—The Harmony of Analogy—The Harmony of Contrasts, - - - - - - - - - 155

CHAPTER VIII.

Transfer Ornaments—How Made, - - - - 162

Monograms—Florentine— Modern — Louis XV.—English. - - - - - - - - 166

Index, - - - - - - - - - 171

THE
COMPLETE CARRIAGE AND WAGON PAINTER.

CHAPTER I.

THE SHOP AND HOW IT SHOULD BE CONSTRUCTED.

Wagon painting, though in some respects inferior to coach painting, is no less an art, and he who would acquire it must give heed to the most minute details, for therein lies his success in finish, and *finish* is the principal point in selling the job or in making a reputation and an extensive business. I do not believe it worth the time to enter into a long explanation of what the paint shop should be, for t is to be supposed that my readers already have their shops built and in use; but it will not be amiss to note a few of the important features which should be and can be made in any shop. Wagon paint shops should be *roomy*, not cut up into small rooms, but large and with high ceilings. A large room in which to do the general work and a smaller room for varnishing is all that is necessary. The varnish room, being almost a sacred place, should be provided with smooth walls and ceiling either of wood or plaster, plenty of light, a water-tight floor, and, of most importance, *a ventilator* in centre of ceiling, running through the roof to the outer air. This feature of a room where varnishing is done is one not fully appreciated by the general class of carriage and wagon builders. There are many, however, who have adopted it, and, once knowing its value, would not be without it. The expense of a ventilator is trifling, and any tinsmith can make one. It consists of a pipe of sheet iron, say fifteen inches in diameter, having upon its outer end—which is run up two feet from the roof—a revolving cap or grating, which, turned by the wind, creates a draught, and that sucks up the dust of the room, and allows the escape of air, deprived of its oxygen, whereby the varnish has an opportunity to harden better.

Varnish dries not so much by the evaporation of its parts as it does by absorbing oxygen from the atmosphere and oxidizing, the oil becoming a sort of resin, and where a goodly supply of fresh air is admitted the quicker and harder the varnish becomes. Windows should be provided with thick curtains—enameled cloth will be found excelent—to enable one to darken the room when the work of the day is complete, to prevent flies from getting upon the work. With these features added to the ready-made paint shop, the painter will be prepared to do his varnishing with no fear of many of the troubles which beset the varnisher, such as "enameling," "pitting," "crawling," etc.

THE FURNITURE OF THE PAINT AND VARNISH ROOMS, BRUSHES, ETC.

The *conveniences* of the paint and varnish rooms, which include trestles, benches, jacks, etc., next demand attention, for these tend to hasten the work, as well as give comfort to the workman. The coach painter requires wheeled trucks on which to move his coach body from place to place, but this is not generally considered necessary in the wagon shop, a body being set up on benches, and allowed to remain so during the painting, then lifted and carried to the varnish room for finishing. Trestles are used for light bodies, or for resting platform gears upon. Benches for placing paint or varnish cups upon when at work and low stools or boxes are necessary for use while striping or lettering. The conventional stone and muller, and perhaps a paint mill, need not be dilated upon, but the *brushes* deserve special mention. Illustrations are presented of those best suited to the wants of the wagon painter. The first to demand attention is the round paint brush, Fig. 1, which is best adapted for laying priming or rough stuff on bodies. The size is that known as 0000 (four naughts).

Fig. 1.—*A Round Paint Brush.*

TO "BRIDLE" A BRUSH.

As the bristles are too long when first purchased, the brush must be "bridled," that is, have an extra binding added. This may be done in several ways: 1. By winding a strong cord around the bristles up to about the middle of the same, or as far from the original binding as desired. 2. By covering one-half the length of the bristles with leather stitched on tightly. 3. By wrapping a piece of muslin or enameled cloth around the bristles, then tying a strong cord around as high as the extra binding should come, turning back the muslin toward the handle, and fastening by tacking to the original binding. 4. There are several patent binders or bridles made of metal in market, and one has an opportunity to choose from these whichever he approves. When the bristles are worn down the bridle may be removed, and a new brush is again in hand.

THE SASH TOOL.

The companion of the round brush is the sash tool, Fig. 2, which is used to "clean up" around moldings and for

Fig. 2.—Sash Tool.

painting small panels. The illustration is so perfect that I refrain from further remark, save to say that the No. 8 tool is about the proper size to purchase. These brushes may be used for painting gears, although we prefer a *flat* bristle brush on such work.

THE CAMEL'S HAIR BRUSH, OR "BLENDER."

For laying colors no better tool can be found than the camel's hair brush, or "blender," as some call them, Fig. 3.

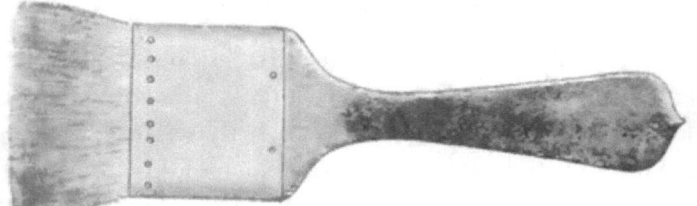

Fig. 3.—Camel's Hair Brush.

I illustrate the proper kind of such a tool and it will be noticed that the hairs are fastened not only by cement, but by riveting through the binding, while those brushes not riveted, shown in Fig. 4, are entirely unfit for any

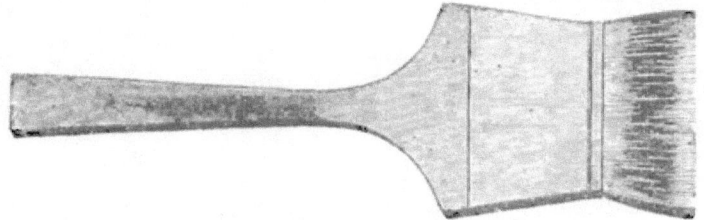

Fig. 4.—A Very Poor Brush.

purpose in the paint shop, and should never be purchased.

THE BADGER HAIR BRUSH.

For laying color and varnish coats the Badger hair brush Fig. 5, is considered best for small panels or any delicate work. It is also used for laying varnish.

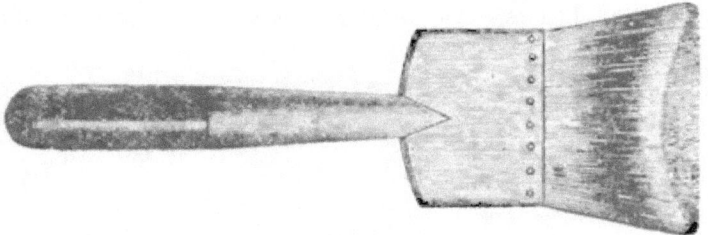

Fig. 5.—Badger Hair Flowing Brush.

The *fitch hair brush* is now almost obsolete, owing to the many imitations which prove worthless.

THE OVAL BRUSH.

For varnishing the large panels of a body or for gears the oval brush, Fig. 6, is best as it will carry a good supply of varnish. These are made of French white bristles *entirely*, and with care will last a long time. A partly worn brush always has the preference over a new one, but the brush-maker now forms the end as if partly worn, which gives it the desired shape and softness.

Fig. 6.—*Oval Varnish Brush, Chiseled.*

CLEANING-UP BRUSH.

A flattened round tool, Fig. 7, is used to "clean up" around moldings, between the spokes, etc. Care should

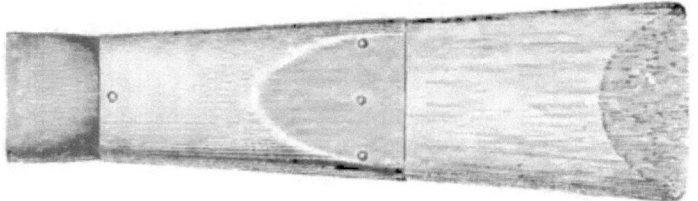

Fig. 7.—*Flattened Round Tool, Chiseled.*

be taken to select brushes having the bristles or hair set in glue, which is insoluble in varnish. Such brushes are far superior to those having the bristles fastened with cement.

With those mentioned and a reasonable supply of flat bristle brushes the shop will be well stocked in the brush line, and we will next look to the pigments or colors to be employed, leaving striping and ornamental pencils for our chapter on such work.

BENCH AND BOXES FOR COLORS.

Having a substantial paint-bench on which to place the "stone" or "flag" and "muller," and upon the end of which a paint mill is secured, we place above it—to be handy—a few shelves, and on these are boxes—cigar boxes will answer—with covers to exclude dust, in which the dry pigments are kept. Upon the front of each box the name of the color contained therein is painted, and the following list comprises all that is required in a wagon paint shop:

LIST OF COLORS REQUIRED IN WAGON PAINTING.

White lead in oil, the best quality ; none other is fit to use.	Chrome yellow. Lemon chrome. Orange chrome. Yellow ochre.	Burnt sienna. Raw umber. Burnt umber. Indian red.
Ultramarine blue.	Raw sienna.	Venetian red.
Dutch pink.	Milori green, L. M. and D.	Prussian blue.
Dry white lead.		Ivory black.
Munich lake.	Chrome green.	Carmine, No. 40.
	Yellow lake.	Vermilion, English, L. and D.
	Whiting.	
	Lamp black.	American vermilion.

and perhaps several others, but as these would form a good beginning, we start from here to mix colors, making mention, first, that the vehicles used are turpentine, brown japan, raw linseed oil (boiled oil is unfit for wagon or carriage work), and the regular list of varnishes, *i.e.*, rubbing and finishing. Prepared paints are perhaps to some a blessing, but he who would use economy in his work must surely mix and grind his own colors. Ready-mixed colors are too expensive for the wagon painter, as, for example, in purchasing French carmine at $10 per lb. he pays at the rate of $10 *per lb. for the japan* in which the pigment is ground, for the average mixture is one pound of dry color and one pound of japan or varnish. Ultramarine blue (dry) can be bought for 25 cents per pound, the japan necessary to make a pound of dry color into paint is worth, say 25 cents, but the price of a pound of ready-prepared ultramarine blue is $1. You can make *two* pounds of paint for 50 cents.

CHAPTER II.

MIXING COLORS.

The simplest mixtures or combination of ingredients are to some the most difficult, and we will first attend to these. Most colors may be mixed with japan and turpentine, adding a very little linseed oil (raw) to give elasticity, and to know exactly what quantity of liquids to use, you may follow these directions:

Lay out on the stone a small quantity of dry pigment and wet it to a mush-like consistency with brown japan; work it well over with the pallette knife and then put it in the mill to grind. Add to the mass in the mill just enough turpentine to liquify it, or make the stiff mass a medium thick liquid, so that it will grind out nicely—if too thin the paint will not readily run through a tight mill, and the mill should be tightened as tight as it is possible to turn it.

When the paint is ground out, add one tablespoonful of raw linseed oil to a pint of paint, stir it well, then test its drying quality by spreading a little upon the thumb nail. Blow the breath upon it to hasten drying, and in a few seconds it will have the same appearance it would have when dry upon the work. If it appear " dead " or " flat," add a little more oil ; if glossy add a little turpentine, and so temper it until it appears to dry upon the nail with an egg-shell gloss, that is, not too dead, nor yet glossy.

The reason why definite amounts of japan, oil or turpentine cannot be stated is owing to the difference in pigments, as for example, umber is a natural dryer and it will neutralize oil to such an extent that more oil may be used than in most any other paint.

Lampblack is of a greasy or anti-drying nature, and consequently requires less oil to form an egg-shell gloss. This plan of mixing may be safely carried on with most pigments.

Vermilion, however, is best mixed with a quick rubbing varnish in the place of japan and no oil whatever should be added to vermilion paint, as it tends to darken it. The quicker you can get vermilion to dry, the better it will hold its color.

Yellow lake and Dutch pink are generally used as glazing colors over green or yellow grounds and therefore should be mixed in varnish instead of oil and japan.

It is quite in keeping with our design to call particular attention to the use of oil. The house-painter places his dependence on oil either raw or boiled, or both, but the wagon or carriage painter would make sorry work if he followed the house-painter in his ideas of durability etc.:—Boiled oil may answer the house-painter's purpose, but it finds no friend in the wagon shop. Japan too, requires looking after; to test it, pour a little on a shallow dish and add a similar quantity of raw linseed oil; if the two amalgamate, the japan may be favorably received, but if the mixture curdles or becomes thick and livery, drop the japan as you would a hot iron.

COMBINING PIGMENTS TO FORM COLORS.

Having explained the manner of mixing paint, let us now look at the combination of pigments to form certain colors. The exact proportions of ingredients cannot be correctly stated, for some pigments vary greatly in their strength or covering power, and again, a shade of color as described, might not suit the eye of all, therefore, we simply tell what pigments to use in making a color, leaving it for the painter to change the proportions to suit his case.

In making tints white-lead forms the base and the colors must be added with care, as some pigments are very strong and a drop will entirely change the tint, while others will hardly be perceptible. To make

1. LEAD COLOR—Take 8 parts white, 1 of blue and 1 of black.

2. MEDIUM GRAY—8 parts white and 2 of black (lampblack).

3. FRENCH GRAY—White tinted with ivory black.

4. LIGHT BUFF—White and yellow ochre.

5. DEEP BUFF—The same with a little Indian red added.

6. GOLD COLOR—White and orange chrome, tinted with red and blue.

7. PEARL COLOR—White, black and red, or white, blue and red.

8. CANARY COLOR—White and lemon yellow.

9. OAK COLOR—White and yellow ochre or raw sienna.

10. OLIVE COLOR—Yellow, blue, black and vermilion.

11. SNUFF COLOR—Yellow and vandyke brown or burnt umber.

12. ROSE COLOR—White and carmine.

13. BOTTLE GREEN—Dutch pink and Prussian blue for ground, glaze with yellow lake.

14. SALMON COLOR—5 parts white, 1 yellow, 1 umber, and 1 red.

15. BROWN—3 parts red, 2 black and 1 yellow.

16. COPPER COLOR—1 part red, 2 yellow and 1 black.

17. LEMON COLOR—5 parts white and 2 lemon yellow.

18. STRAW COLOR—Same, with a drop or two of vermilion.

19. FAWN COLOR—8 parts white, 1 red, 2 yellow and 1 burnt umber.

20. FLESH COLOR—8 parts white, 3 vermilion, 3 chrome yellow.

21. CHESTNUT COLOR—2 parts red, 2 chrome yellow, 1 black.

22. WINE COLOR—2 parts ultramarine blue, 3 carmine.

23. MAROON YELLOW—3 parts carmine, 2 yellow.

24. TAN COLOR—5 parts burnt sienna, 2 yellow, 1 raw umber.

25. PEA GREEN—5 parts white and 1 chrome green.

26. CITRON COLOR—3 parts red, 2 yellow and 1 blue.

27. STONE COLOR—5 parts white, 2 yellow and 1 burnt umber.

28. DRAB COLOR—9 parts white and 1 burnt umber.

29. LILAC COLOR—4 parts red, 3 white and 1 blue.

30. PURPLE COLOR—Same, with more blue.

31. VIOLET COLOR—Same, with more red.

32. LONDON SMOKE—2 parts umber, 1 white and 1 red.

33. CREAM COLOR—5 parts white, 2 yellow and 1 red.

34. CLARET COLOR—Red and black or carmine and blue.

35. DOVE COLOR—Red, white, blue and yellow.

36. LIGHT GRAY—9 parts white, 1 blue and 1 black.

37. WILLOW GREEN—5 parts white and 1 verdigris (tube color).

38. PEACH BLOSSOM—8 parts white, 1 blue, 1 red and 1 yellow.

39. BRONZE GREEN—5 parts chrome green, 1 black and 1 umber.

40. CARNATION RED—Carmine and white, or Munich lake and white.

41. GRASS GREEN—3 parts yellow and 1 Prussian blue.

42. BRICK COLOR—2 parts yellow ochre, 1 red and 1 white.

43. PORTLAND STONE—3 parts raw umber, 3 yellow ochre and 1 white.

44. PLUM COLOR—3 parts white, 1 blue and 1 red.

45. FRENCH RED—Indian red and vermilion—glazed with carmine.

46. CHOCOLATE COLOR—Indian red, black and yellow.

47. YELLOW LAKE—Umber and white, equal parts; add yellow and lake.

48. OLIVE BROWN—1 part lemon yellow and 3 burnt umber.

49. CLAY DRAB—Raw sienna, raw umber and white.

50. BISMARCK BROWN—1 oz. carmine, ½ oz. crimson lake, 1 oz. best gold bronze. If desired lighter, use vermilion in place of the carmine.

51. JONQUIL YELLOW—Flake white (tube color), chrome yellow and a very little vermilion or carmine.

52. CHAMOLINE—A new color, so named because it resembles in color that of a chamois skin when wet. Mix lemon chrome, 1 part; raw sienna, 3 parts; and white about 5 parts, until the approximate shade is reached.

53. DARK MILORI GREEN is specially adapted for

wagon bodies. It makes a very rich panel color, superior to Prussian blue, green, or chrome green, or mixtures of blue and yellow.

54. TEA GREEN is made by mixing raw umber, blue and chrome green. It makes a rich panel-color, and, with a sample of tea before him, the painter can easily get the proper shade.

55. WILLOW-LEAF GREEN—A very light yellowish shade of olive, yellow, blue, black and red.

56. PRIMROSE YELLOW—White and King's yellow, a noted English color, but not much used in this country.

57. LE CUIR OR LEATHER COLOR—One part burnt umber and two parts burnt sienna, then tone with white.

58. JAPAN BROWN—Black japan mixed with vermilion.

59. DARK RICH BROWNS—Take Indian red, five parts, and Prussian blue, one part; grind, and mix in brown Japan and turpentine and add a very little oil. By changing the proportions of ingredients the color can be made light or dark as desired. Vermilion and black will make a very nice brown, but we believe that all red-and-black browns are softened and improved in tone by the addition of yellow. Umber brown without the addition of red is a cold, raw color, unless placed beside a red ground or stripe.

GLAZING.

GLAZING is the term given to a transparent coating put over a similar colored ground, as carmine over reds, or yellow lake over yellow or green, or verdigris over green. Many shades of *lake* may be made by glazing with carmine, and there are many who never employ *lake pigments* in their work, owing to its tendency to fade or to flake off. The ground being made with Indian red and black, according as the shade of lake is to be light or dark, a glaze of carmine will produce a beautiful color and one that will be durable. Rich blues are made by glazing Prussian blue lightened with white with ultramarine. Glazing is simply the dry pigment ground in rubbing varnish, no oil, no japan nor turpentine being used, and it is put on in a similar manner to varnish, care being taken not to have clouds or runs in the work.

In mixing colors, it is the custom of some painters to lay out upon the stone the requisite quantity of various pigments, and then mix and grind the mass in the mill, but by this means dull or "lifeless" colors are produced. To do this properly the required pigments for a given color should be mixed and ground separately, then the proper proportions may be put together and thoroughly mixed. By this means all the freshness of the color will be retained, a more perfect commingling of the particles will be insured, and there will be less liability of separation in the cup, or settling of one heavy pigment from the others, which is sure to destroy the uniformity of coloring.

VERMILION should not be ground fine in the mill, for not only does the iron surfaces with which it comes in contact injure the color, but the crushing of the grains brings about an orange tinge which is decidedly objectionable.

LIGHT ENGLISH VERMILION has the greatest body or covering power, and is used for striping and lettering, while the *Deep* English vermilion is better suited for coloring gears or panels.

American vermilion and white lead forms a peach blossom pink which makes an **excellent ground for English vermilion.**

IVORY BLACK—Many purchase prepared black with the expectation of getting an article ready for spreading with the brush, and when they find that the paint is *too thick* and requires thinning to a proper consistency for the work in hand, they are at a loss what to do with it—whether to add oil, turpentine, varnish or Japan—and in some cases the paint is spoiled by the vehicle used to dilute it. To such we would say: take from the can the required amount of black, and add just sufficient turpentine to soften it or thin it to a cream-like consistency, stirring it meanwhile with a flattened stick. Next add a very small quantity of raw oil and test it on the thumb nail until it dries *not too dead*. Be careful not to use too much oil, for too much is worse than none at all, while the proper quantity gives ease in spreading and durability to the work.

PUTTY.

The next in order is PUTTY, and as there are several kinds for the several purposes we will give recipes for each. Putty should be tempered with either oil, varnish, or japan, according to the purposes to which it is put. These are:

First.—WHITE PUTTY, composed of keg lead and dry lead and whiting. The dry pigments are beaten and worked into the keg lead until of a putty consistency, then a little brown japan is added to cause it to dry well, and a little more whiting is worked in to bring about a stiff putty for filling holes, leaving it softer for filling the grain of ash, etc.

Second.—QUICK PUTTY—Take dry lead and whiting,

equal parts, and mix to putty with equal parts brown japan and rubbing varnish.

Third.--BLACK PUTTY—For hurried work mix the same as quick putty, using lampblack in place of whiting.

Fourth.—BLACK PUTTY FOR IRONS—To be used where the iron work does not fit the wood. Mix three-fourths lampblack with one-fourth dry lead or whiting, with japan.

Fifth.—BLACK BEDDING PUTTY—For glass frames mix lampblack and whiting in equal parts (bulk) with equal parts of rubbing varnish and japan to a soft putty consistency. Then having some black velvet or plush at hand, unravel it so as to secure the short fibres of the material, which, when mixed with the putty in the same manner as hair is mixed with plaster, will bind it firmly together and no jar of the vehicle will cause it to crack and fly out. This putty is excellent for bedding the glasses of hearses and is used by most hearse builders in preference to any other.

The ordinary putty of the glazier finds no place in a wagon paint shop.

It is a good plan to color putty to a color similar to the job; as, for example, if the job is to be red, add a little red to the putty; if green, add green, and so on.

CHAPTER III.

PRIMING.

Having our shop tools and paints ready for use and being somewhat acquainted with the mixing of paints of various colors, we will take for the first lesson in painting a platform geared business wagon with ribbed body and panel top.

There are several methods of reaching a final finish, and it will be well to glance at each. Then he who chooses to follow one path may do so, while his neighbor can take another.

LEAD COLOR METHOD.

First comes the old or lead color method. As soon as the body, wheels and bars are completed by the woodworker, a coat of priming should be put on to prevent the raising of the grain of the wood. This priming is made of pure linseed oil, slightly colored with white lead. A small quantity of brown japan may be added to hasten the drying, though some prefer to omit the drier when time is of no account. The oil of the priming is the main dependence. It is soaked into the pores of the wood and partly seals them against the entrance of moisture while the small grains of lead partially close up the largest pores.

The tread of the wheel should be coated, as that prevents the swelling of the rim or felloe, while the tire is being put on. Just here let me remark that a tire should never be so hot as to scorch or char the wood. There is no necessity for it, and a careful workman will not permit it.

The spring bars or blocks should be coated all over. The coating now put on acts as a preventive coat, as shown above. When it is dry the work is ready for the smith.

The body will not be wanted at once, so we can prime it with some kind of paint, all over, excepting the floor. Some simply prime the outside, leaving the inside unpainted for the time. That is an error, for the bare wood is apt to absorb dampness and the broad side panels are liable to check. The priming being allowed from 36 to 48 hours for drying, it may then receive a good sandpapering with No. 2 sandpaper. The largest nail holes may then be puttied with putty made as per formula No. 1, previously spoken of, leaving the small holes to be partly filled with paint. Dust off clean and apply,

THE FIRST COAT OF LEAD.

This paint may be mixed as follows : Take from the keg the required amount of white lead, say, two pounds, and make into a paste-like consistency with raw oil ; then add one-half as much brown japan, and finally, thin to a working consistency with turpentine. Lay this paint on as evenly and sparingly as possible to cover the ground, for a thick coating is not desirable. Rub it into the wood as well as you can with the brush and stand the job aside to dry.

When this coat is dry, it will be best to go over every part of the frame, seat raisers, etc., which are of hard wood, and plaster the grain full of soft putty as per formula No. 2. This being quick drying, may be sandpapered in an hour or so. The sandpaper used in scouring the priming coat will be good enough for this work, as it is not our desire to cut through the paint, but to simply smooth it. Many err in this; they apply a coat of paint, and then sandpaper it nearly all off again, which is just so much time and material wasted. The rule should be to first make the job smooth, and then apply the paint in as neat and clean a manner as possible, avoiding all necessity for hard sandpapering.

ROUGH-STUFFING THE PANELS.

On extra fine wagon work the body panels are coated with rough-stuff and rubbed with pumice stone; but for ordinary work this is not necessary. But the large side panels may be rough-stuffed, and we will now look for the best mixture for the purpose.

Fire proof paint, Grafton paint, Ohio paint, and English filling are all one and the same thing; the latter being simply Grafton paint exported to England, there colored, and returned to this country as "English filling," and the price quadrupled.

Procure either of these, with an equal quantity, by weight, of keg lead, and mix with equal parts of brown japan and rubbing varnish. Run it through the mill loosely and thin it to work nicely, with turpentine. No better rough-stuff can be had. The only advantage gained in using prepared rough-stuff is that by being mixed in large quantities it is apt to be more uniform than that mixed by the painter. Rough-stuff should not be applied thick, like mud, but should receive as much care in its application as any other paint. If it be put on thick, and with brush-marks showing, the finish will show the marks just as plainly.

The purpose in using rough-stuff is to produce a surface

having sufficient grit to cause it to level down nicely by rubbing it with lump pumice stone. For wagon work, two coats are generally sufficient, but on carriage work as many as five are sometimes applied. The coat of rough-stuff having been put on as directed, give it from 24 to 48 hours to dry; then apply the second coat. No preparations, such as sandpapering, etc., need be made; simply dust off the job and apply the paint.

It is the best plan, to let the smith have the body while in rough-stuff, for then if he burns or bruises any part, it can be readily repaired before the "rubbing down" is begun.

The ironing of the gears and body being now completed, we will take in hand the gears, which, up to the present, have received the priming or preventive coat only.

LEADING THE GEARS.

Slipping out the king-bolt, we run the front platform from under the body, and then, resting the front on the barrel, and the hind axle on benches, we remove the hind wheels, leaving the body in a position to be worked at conveniently. The gears now receive a good "cutting down" with coarse sandpaper, until but little of the priming coat is discerned, and, after a good dusting, these parts are ready for the *lead*. As we are about to paint the gears with English vermilion, it will be well to apply a pink or peach-blossom paint to serve for a ground work; therefore, we mix keg lead with oil to a thick mass, and stir in enough Venetian red, or American vermilion, to form a clean pink color; then, add one-half as much brown Japan as you used of the oil. stir well, and run through the mill. Next, thin with turpentine and apply as evenly as possible to every part of the gears, the *under side* as well as other parts. Clean up nicely around the butts of spokes, nuts bolt-heads, etc., and stand aside for drying.

The body having been looked over, and all bruised places repaired with putty, is in condition for rubbing, so selecting several pieces of pumice stone, and preparing a pail of clean water, a sponge, chamois skin and a water tool, begin the

RUBBING OUT OF ROUGH-STUFF.

There seems to be nothing so well adapted for rubbing the surface of paint, preparatory to laying on the finer coats of color, etc., as pumice-stone (the lava thrown from volcanoes). It is porous, inexpensive, and possesses admirable frictional properties. The first of these qualities renders it excellent as a rubber; its porosity allows it to cleanse itself, or, in other words, the refuse rubbed from the surface of the paint lodges in the pores, while the projecting portions continue to cut, and the application of water removes from the pores the refuse. If, of good quality, it cuts down the paint rapidly, and a clean cutting surface is exposed to the paint at all times. Pumice stone, however, lacks uniformity; some lumps being heavy, with closed pores, presenting a stone-like appearance, while others are light and open-grained. The latter is the best. The stone, when selected, should first be dipped in water, that its grain may easily be seen, and then cut with an old saw across the grain, so that the pores may retain as fully as possible their clearing and cutting qualities. Large pieces should be used when practicable, so as not to rub the surface into hollows.

There is another species of stone much used for rubbing rough-stuff, and known as "English rubbing stone." It is a sort of sandstone of fine quality, and is a greater absorbent of water than pumice or other qualities of sand stone. It must be kept in a damp place, otherwise it becomes hard and flinty. For rough work this stone may answer a good purpose, but it is almost too coarse for fine work. There is also in the market a prepared brick or stone, of German origin, branded with the name of *Schumachersche Fabrik*. (It may have been originally intended as a whetstone for shoemakers.) It is used by many first-class builders, and has superseded lump pumice in a measure, although it will never entirely take its place.

The stone having been chosen according to the conditions explained above, or as nearly as circumstances will permit, the pieces should be cut and smoothed by rubbing them upon a flat stone. The stone should set nicely to the surface and be moved either in circles as in polishing, or lengthwise of the panel, pressing firmly upon it, but not too hard, for it would then rag or tear up the paint. Plenty of water must be used to prevent heating. It is the practice of many to apply a "guide coat" or "stain" over the rough stuff (this is simply a mixture of dry pigment and japan and turpentine, put on very thin) to enable the rubber to see when he has rubbed the surface level, as when all the "stain" is rubbed off the surface should be perfect. As the work continues, the stone should be pressed more and more lightly, and more water should be used, in order that all fine scratches may be removed. When the "rubbing out" is completed, wash the job , using the water tool (a common sash-tool) to clean out corners, etc., then dry off with a chamois skin, and stand the job aside for the evaporation of any moisture which may remain in the pores of the paint.

PUTTING THE FINAL FOUNDATION COAT ON THE GEARS.

The gears we left in pink colored lead to dry, and these must now receive attention. Putty for this job should be made as follows: Take equal parts (bulk) of keg lead and whiting, and beat the whiting into the lead with a wooden mallet, until the mass is of a putty consistency; add a little red, and a very little brown japan and knead all together nicely. Next go over every part and putty up all holes or imperfections, and plaster the fronts of spokes and any other open-grained places. When this is dry, which will be perhaps in an hour or two, smooth down all parts, particularly the putty, with partly worn sandpaper, dust off, and apply a coat of the following mixture: Take keg lead and mix it to a soft paste with turpentine, add one gill of brown japan to every pint of paint, then color it by the addition of American vermilion. It will do no harm, and add greatly to the durability of the work to add say, a tablespoonful of raw oil, but if the job must be hurried this may be omitted. This being the final coat of the foundation, it should be applied as smoothly as possible, and the under parts need not receive this coating.

PAINTING THE BODY.

The body now being dry, take the finest sandpaper and gently rub over the rubbed portion, and nicely prepare the ribs, etc., for color. It is customary with some painters to lay on a ground coat of some color corresponding with the hue of the color the job is to be painted, but this is not positively necessary, for its purpose is merely to economize time and expensive color. With the exception of a few extra fine or transparent colors, which are intensified or made more brilliant by application over particular grounds, the color may just as well be laid directly on the rough-stuff or lead surface. This job we will paint green panels, black ribs, and black top sides, with name panel in vermilion, glazed with carmine. The color for the panels will be best perhaps, if we use deep Milori green, or we may use chrome green deepened with Prussian blue, whichever is at hand.

Milori green, however, makes the richest color, and it may be mixed as we have before directed, *i.e.*, mix and grind in brown japan, thin with turpentine ; then add one tablespoonful of raw linseed oil to every pint of paint. The name panel or belt may be coated with light English vermilion this time, as that covers better than the deep and the top, sides, etc., may have a coat of lampblack. These colors must be laid on with camel's hair brushes to have them as thin and smooth as can be, and in painting the body panels the ribs should receive as much attention as the panel, no matter if they are ultimately to be in black. The inside of the body may at this time be painted with a light pea green.

While the body is drying we will lightly sandpaper the gears, and apply a coat of American vermilion, using a flat bristle brush and sash tool. This forms a good ground for the English vermilion, which will be the next in order. The ends of the hubs, and the ends of the pole or shafts need not be painted with the vermilion, for those parts will be "blacked off."

THE SECOND COAT ON THE BODY.

A second coat of color is now in order on the body, having allowed several hours for drying. A good "mossing off" that is rubbing over the surface of paint with a bunch of moss or curled hair, prepares it for color. Milori green on body panels. Deep English vermilion on name panel or belt, and ivory black on top. Give at least five hours for drying, then apply color and varnish, which is made by adding to rubbing varnish a sufficient amount of the color to slightly stain it. This preserves the freshness of the color. The green, the red, and the black must all be done alike, and varnish brushes should be used for this work. It is as necessary to use care in applying color and varnish to have it clean, and without runs, as if applying a finishing coat of varnish, for if it be well done there will be less rubbing to do in finishing, and a better job will result. Some slap on color and varnish with the thought "it has to be rubbed smooth," but that is not the proper way and the thought and aim should be to see "how nicely I can put on this coat."

PAINTING THE GEARS.

The color and varnish on the body, let us now color the gears. Rubbing over every part with fine sandpaper or curled hair, we mix English vermilion (deep), as before directed, and apply a nice, even coat over all, bottom of axles, springs, etc., as well as the top; stand the work aside to dry, which will be perhaps two hours; then put on a heavy coat of color and varnish—made by adding a little of the vermilion color to rubbing varnish.

The whole job is now in color and varnish, and, when dry (say after 48 hours, if not hurried), the rubbing of the body with pulverized pumice stone is in order. The gears do not require rubbing with pumice; they may be "haired off" preparatory to striping.

Procuring some pulverized pumice stone—the grade best suited is known as No. 12, No. 14 being finer—some pieces of woolen cloth for "rub-rags," clean water, sponge, chamois skin and water-tool we are ready for

THE RUBBING PROCESS.

To do this nicely, begin on the upper part of the body and work downward. First fold the rub-rag into several folds or thicknesses, and saturate it well with water, dip it into the ground pumice and then begin the work of rubbing. Bear on quite hard, and keep the rag well wet and also well supplied with the pumice powder. Pass your finger over the parts rubbed, occasionally, to see whether you have yet made the surface smooth; if so wash off the panel and dry it with the chamois. Proceed in like manner over all until the body has a clean egg-shell gloss, and appears perfectly free from pits or specks. When this is done the job is ready for lettering, excepting the name panel, which is yet to be glazed with carmine. This we will do at once. Grind a small quantity of carmine No. 40 in rubbing varnish, then dilute it with more of the same varnish, and apply a flowing coat in the same manner as clear varnish, being careful not to have runs, clouds, or heavy flows.

This done, and the inside having been second-coated with pea green, we can say the painting is complete.

The gears being rubbed with curled hair or moss, are ready for striping, and we will leave them for the present to give directions for bringing up a job to this point by another process.

CHAPTER IV.

THE PUTTY KNIFE METHOD.

When the priming and first coat of lead, as previously described are dry, mix some keg-lead with turpentine and japan, equal parts, add a very little lampblack, or red, or green, according to the color the job is to be painted, making the paint a stiff paste or soft putty consistency. With a stiff brush spread this on to a small portion of the body, say: four panels. It will then be noticed that as fast as the turpentine evaporates, the paint will become "dead" in appearance, and when quite dead or "flat," take a broad bladed putty-knife and plaster over, the same as if it were putty; pressing the paint into the pores and inequalities of the wood, and scraping off all that is not required to so fill up. Go on in this manner until the body has all been passed over, and set the job aside to dry. The gears may be done in a similar manner, using a stout piece of harness leather for rubbing the paint on spokes and other round places. When this plaster coat is dry, cut it down nicely with sandpaper, and apply the color direct; then color and varnish. This is a much cheaper plan than rough-stuffing, and when well done, the job will look nearly as well.

ANOTHER WAY.

An improved plan is to mix with the plastering paint, one-half the bulk of Wheeler's Patent Wood Filler, a mixture of silica or flint, which, when ground fine, forms small angular grains or needle-like pieces, which adhere to wood very firmly, and being impervious to any liquid, completely seal up the pores of wood against the admission of moisture, or the oil from subsequent coats.

THE WOOD FILLING METHOD.

The body having been completed, no further than the frame-work, it receives a priming of wood filling. The chamfers and faces of the rails or ribs are then plastered with hard-drying putty and sandpapered, being then ready for color. The panels are got out and smoothed by the body maker, being left from $\frac{1}{2}$ to $\frac{3}{4}$ of an inch wider than necessary to fit the body, to allow for shrinkage. These then receive wood filling, which is applied freely and immediately wiped over with rags, until no *surface coating* is left, nearly all the filling having penetrated the wood. Give two days for drying, and then apply rough-stuff made as follows: Grafton paint or Eng. filling 3 parts, white lead (keg) 2 parts, oil japan 2 parts, rubbing varnish 1 part: dilute with turpentine. For the first coat add a tablespoonful of oil to a pint of paint, because that which comes next to the elastic priming must be more elastic than the subsequent coats. A period of 48 hours must now be allowed for the first coat of roughstuff to dry, after which two coats without oil in the mixture may be applied each day. Give one day for the stain or guide coat to dry, and then rub down as before described. The panels may now be fitted to their places, screwing them fast from the inside, thus leaving the outside of the body in good order for color.

We specially recommend this method of rough-stuffing the panels before they are fitted, inasmuch as that part between the panel and rib is thus well painted, allowing no chance of injury by water entering at those places ; and besides, it allows of making a smooth job with less labor.

The gears having been similarly primed with wood filling, and the smith having completed his work upon them, the first operation is a good cutting down with No. 3 sandpaper, which prepares the work for a coat of lead— pure keg lead, mixed with oil, japan and turpentine. When this is dry, the puttying up of all open-grained places and holes are in order. The second coat of lead paint, containing a little chrome yellow and a trifling amount of vermilion to form a rich cream color, is next applied. Two coats of this will suffice for the color, when color and varnish should be put on. When this is dry, moss off for striping.

Having brought the wagon up to the striping, lettering, and ornamenting we will now take a retrospective view and note the particular points not so fully explained heretofore.

VARNISHING.

The varnishing of a carriage body is a very delicate operation, and requires a considerable amount of practical knowledge on the part of the workman, if he would produce satisfactory results. But it is not so difficult to varnish a wagon body, notwithstanding. To those not accustomed to this class of work, it seems a big job to varnish the sides of a large furniture van, for instance, which spreads over a surface of 120 square feet, or an animal cage of a little less surface, but it is quite easily done with proper facilities. The brushes used for such work are flat ones, "double thick" 4 inches wide, of French bristles. The workman begins at one end, laying on the varnish up and down, and "finishing up" as he proceeds lap after lap the width of the brush. With quick setting varnish two men are put to work, one laying on the varnish, the other finishing up.

On ordinary business wagons, trucks, etc., much more care is given to the final finish than was the case a few years ago, and in some shops expert carriage varnishers have been employed in order to turn out extra jobs. So to carry out our plan of making a first-class job we will go into minute details regarding the

VARNISHING OF WAGONS AND SLEIGHS.

So far as the room is concerned, we will say but little, as we have already touched on that subject. In the first place the room should be provided with a heating arrangement by which a uniform degree of heat may be maintained, and where no other means can be resorted to, a large self-feeding stove should be put up, although it is best to have the stove in the paint room and close to the partition of the varnish room, the partition at that place being made of sheet iron. This will generally suffice to heat both rooms. The room should be free from everything not necessary for the job in hand, for dust will accumulate on pictures or other wall hangings to the detriment of the work. The rubbing with pumice-stone, and the cleaning of the body should be done in the paint rooms, for we do not want the floor of the varnish room soaked with water—not even sprinkled—for the evaporation of moisture from the floor is very apt to cause "pitting," "enameling," and other difficulties. The rubbing coats of varnish, that is the color-and-varnish, and the clear rubbing varnish, over the lettering, and striping,—having been applied with as much care as if a **finishing coat, the** final rubbing is now in order. The rubbing or leveling of varnish with pulverized pumice stone and water bears an important part in the work of making a fine finish.

Finish each part as you proceed, leaving a nice clean surface, well washed and shammied. The work of rubbing done, carry the body to the varnish room and set it upon barrels or boxes as before; then with a large round duster —one kept for the varnish room—give the body a thorough dusting. It is a good plan to moisten the palm of the hand with finishing varnish, and then to pass the end of the duster over it to slightly moisten the bristles, which enables it to pick up any lint left by the shammy.

Fig. 8.—Standard Varnish Brushes.

For most jobs the flat bristle brush is considered best. They are furnished in sets, and the bristles should be set in glue.

The varnisher, now having everything ready, the work of laying on the varnish is begun. The pumice stone should be well examined to discover if any grains of grit or sand are in it, for sometimes one scratch across a panel will disfigure the whole job. The rub-rag, sponge, shammy, water, etc., should all be as clean as possible—

and by all means see to it that neither the pail, sponge nor shammy have been used for washing the hands. In rubbing, the pumice powder must not be allowed to dry on the work, but must be kept wet, or washed off frequently. In beginning a panel, first pass the wet sponge over it to take off any dust there may be upon it, then seek the roughest portions and give particular attention to them; the smoother parts will be passed over often enough to level them without that especial care. All sharp edges and moldings should be slighted, or they may be cut through, which would necessitate touching up, and that requires time, while the job is not improved thereby. It would be a useless task for us to direct the manner of varnishing—suffice it to say, go at the work with confidence in your ability to do it properly. Flow on the varnish plentifully,—a sparse coat will not make a good job— lay off the large panels with up and down strokes of the brush, let it set a moment, then with a sharpened whalebone go over and pick out any specks that are seen, and then immediately run the brush from bottom to top very lightly to finish. Go all over the job in this manner and you may rest assured that your work will come out all right.

The gears may be varnished in the paint room, providing there is not room enough in the varnish room, for these do not require so much care. However, they should receive a goodly share of varnish, and this brings us to the finish of the work. We will now look at some of the ills that beset the painter.

SWEATING.

Sweating of varnish is liable to occur after it has been rubbed and allowed to stand a while. This is caused by the varnish not having had proper time for drying. Proper care is not taken, at times, to lay the rubbing coats as they should be : they are applied too heavy or with specks and brush marks showing, and to get the surface smooth too much rubbing has to be done ; then the varnish will probably *sweat*. To overcome this, rub the job lightly with pumice stone and apply the varnish immediately before the surface has time to sweat. But when time can conveniently be given for the varnish to become hard it is certainly best.

Varnish that has " sweated out " if varnished over without first rubbing the sweaty gloss off is liable to cause pitting, or pinholing, and enameling, three of the worst evils that the paint shop is heir to.

CLEANING NEW BRUSHES.

To clean a new varnish brush, hold it over a piece of enameled cloth or patent leather, and work the dry bristles in the hands so long as there is seen any little white specks coming from it, then dip it in rubbing varnish and use on common work until you are sure the dirt is all out. Never wash a brush in turpentine if it can be avoided. If a brush gets dirty by a fall to the floor, hold it up with the bristles pointing downward, and pour turpentine over it, allowing it to run off carrying the dirt with it. Keep your varnish brushes suspended in varnish—or, what is better, get from the varnish-maker some finishing varnish made with *no driers in it*. This will keep your brushes in good condition for years, and never give trouble in varnishing.

CHAPTER V.

THE CARE OF MATERIALS.

Keep paint brushes suspended in water, allowing th water to come just over the lower part of the binding. In winter throw a handful of salt into the water to keep it from freezing. A shop should be supplied with a sufficient number of brushes, so that it will not be necessary to change one from one color to another, except in rare cases.

Pumice-stone should be kept in a covered box to exclude dust, for a job may be ruined by a single scratch caused by some foreign subtance in the pumice.

FAILURES IN VARNISHING.

Failure to make a good job of varnishing may sometimes be traced to one of the following causes, viz.: When the pail or bucket is used for holding the water with which the hands are washed from oil and dirt.

When the chamois (shammy) has been rinsed in greasy and dirty water, or been used as a towel.

When the sponge has been used in a similar manner.

When the water is not perfectly clean and free from grease or soap.

When the duster has been used for dusting paint, and is not in a clean condition.

When the cups are besmeared with dried or gummy varnish, or not otherwise clean.

When the brushes are not kept in a covered brush-keeper, or are suspended in liquid other than varnish, or are dirty around the binding and handle, or lousy.

When the varnish room is used for all sorts of work, is not clean, the floor wet, the room not kept at a uniform degree of heat, and is not free from everything not necessary in varnishing the job.

When the painter has undertaken a job that he is not competent to carry through.

When the varnish is not perfect, either in age or manufacture, or of the quality required to do a first-class job.

TROUBLES OF THE PAINTER.

Many are greatly troubled at times with their paint or varnish, and it is now our duty to enumerate some of these annoyances, and to explain why they occur and how to cure them.

SPECKY VARNISHES.

We sometimes have a job that looks as if a salt sprinkler had been shaken over it before the varnish was dry. It is full of little specks. Assured that there was no dust in the room, none in the brushes and no pumice-stone on the work, where shall we look? Why, at your varnish! It has been in a cold or damp place; the can was kept on the the floor (the coldest part of the room), and the varnish has become chilled, which has caused a separation of the driers from the oil, and the result is "specks." To cure the evil, set the can of varnish on two bricks upon the stove and warm it gradually; don't overheat it; then, *always* keep your varnish cans on a shelf up over the heater, where it is warm.

CRAWLING OF PAINT OR VARNISH.

When the paint or varnish draws up, and won't stay

where it is put, it is called "crawling." This may occur if the under coat or surface is too glossy, or if the paint has grown fat by being run through a heated mill; or if the surface be chilled, or when there is grease or soap on the surface.

Varnish is liable to crawl when put over an old though well rubbed surface of English varnish, and to remedy the evil, first apply a very thin coat of japan and turpentine equal parts, then apply the varnish over that, and it will not crawl.

To prevent paint from crawling, wipe the surface with a damp shammy, or better wash the whole job and shammy it dry. Crawling on lake stripes is often seen, but the damp shammy rubbed over it will generally stop it.

BLISTERING.

The blistering of a varnished surface after the varnish has had ample time to dry thoroughly, is we believe, due entirely to the evaporation of moisture which lies confined under the varnish. We never see blisters occur unless there is excessive heat upon the surface, and heat causes the evaporation of the confined moisture, which in turn raises the varnish, which has become soft by the heat, into puff-balls and blisters. Much of this is due to unseasoned wood, and much more to moisture sealed up in the rough-stuff coats. The water used in rubbing penetrates the porous paint, and many times, the job being in a hurry, a coat of paint is put over it before the moisture has dried out, and blistering follows. Boiled oil is frequently the cause of blisters, for that, drying, as it does, on the outside, and remaining soft underneath, deceives the painter, and other coats go over it, drying hard, and when a hot sun strikes the job, blisters follow.

CRACKING OF PAINT AND VARNISH.

A coat of paint which dries quickly and hard, put over an oily paint not quite hard, will cause cracking. It may not be seen until long after the job is finished, and it may be that large cracks will appear, or there may be "fire-checks" that is, thousands of exceedingly fine cracks running in every direction. Almost all cracking of paint or varnish arises from this carelessness in putting one coat over another as above mentioned. Again, cracking may follow where a ready prepared paint was used, which, in order to cheapen it, was well dosed by the paint factor with chemicals, which act when coming in contact with oil, and form soap, which will never dry hard, and then the subsequent coats will open out into cracks.

TO PAINT CANVAS-TOP SIDES.

The standing sides of a business wagon top and the roof may be painted in an excellent manner as follows: First, mix some rye flour paste, the same as that used for paper-hanging, and give the canvas a good coat of it inside and out. Allow plenty of time for drying; then with new, clean sandpaper gently rub over to take off any nibs, etc. Next, mix white lead with japan and a little oil, say one-third as much oil as japan, thin with turpentine and give three coats, lightly sandpapering between each coat. Finish with white color and varnish, rub off with pumice, letter, etc., and finish with body finishing varnish. The curtains should not be prepared with paste, but may be tacked up to the wall and receive the same paint as is put on the sides and roof. They require to be flexible, and the paste would stiffen them. This plan saves paint, makes a smooth job, and a durable one as well

GLAZING WITH CARMINE.

Carmine gears and panels have frequently to be made in the wagon shop, and it is no easy task even for the experienced painter to finish such work without clouds or streaks; therefore we believe the inexperienced may need some explanation of the way to do this work.

First get the ground solid and well-rubbed out of color, and varnish (glazing on dead color seldom makes a good job), vermilion, Indian red, or whatever the shade of red, no matter. Then crush the lumps of carmine on the stone, mix in rubbing varnish and grind through the mill the same as any other color, being sure to have it just as fine as the mill can make it. Next, add more varnish until the color or glaze is not *too strong*. Slow-drying, rubbing or finishing gear varnish is best. Now dust off the gear or the panel nicely, and flow on a good heavy coat; if a wheel, do only two or three spokes at a time, and be careful not to get any glazing on hub or rim; continue thus, finishing the rim last. Any lap you make will be seen, so don't make any. If it be a panel that you are working on, act with the glazing the same as if it was a finishing coat of clear varnish.

Some attempt to flow a wheel all over, and then "lay it off," but in nine cases out of ten they "get stuck;" the safe way is the best. Do not take any risks with carmine, for it is an expensive color, and washing off a clouded job is not a pleasant task.

On cheap work, Munich lake may be substituted for carmine, and but few can tell the difference when the glazing is done properly. Glazing should be saved, *i. e.* kept in a well-stoppered bottle, and it may be used for striping or for the next job. Don't throw it away.

CHAPTER VI.

WAGON STRIPING.

"That appears easy enough!" exclaimed a visitor to our paint shop one day, while looking at one of the workmen engaged in striping a gear. And so it is—with the proviso—*if you know how.*

Striping is an art acquired only by long practice; one may look on for years, and then not be able to draw a straight line. Again, many suppose that to stripe well the workman must have a very steady hand, which is true only in part; a steady hand or quiet nerve is certainly desirable, but it is not that only; *the eye* must do its share of work, and the larger portion falls upon it. The eye must be quicker than the hand, to detect any variation from the true path, and then, the brain telegraphs to the fingers to change the movement before a mark has been made.

The mechanical work of striping may be easily acquired; but the artistic and inventive part must emanate from an inborn taste, or in short, from the brain of a ' natural genius." We might go on indefinitely and illustrate fancy striping for the benefit of those who will not try to make their own designs; but we do not care to do so, and our aim is simply to show the general style of wagon striping, with explanations regarding the tools and materials used, leaving our readers to take their cue from these and then invent and put on their own ideas of a stripe. We will begin with

THE STRIPER'S KIT OF TOOLS.

Striping pencils are made of hair fastened into various sized quills, or to wood, and there are a few made with a tin ferrule, but these are apt to cut the hair, and consequently they soon go to pieces and are of no account. Sable-hair pencils are the most expensive, ranging in price from 50 cts. to $8 each; they are made from the hair on the tip of the tail of the sable martin (an animal of the weasel family) and it is the scarcity of the hair which creates the high price.

A sable pencil for fine lines, where heavy color like white lead is used, is excellent, as it is sufficiently elastic to hold up the color and yet make a clear, full stripe. There are two kinds of sable hair, the red and the black, either of which will make good stripes; but the red hair is more extensively used for artists' pencils, owing to its shortness, being seldom over three-quarters of an inch in length.

Camel's-hair pencils are made in the same manner, *i. e.*, in quills and fastened to wood. The hair is much softer than sable, and for this reason, as well as their low price, they are universally preferred.

STRIPING PENCILS.

Striping pencils are made in many sizes and designated by numbers by the manufacturers, from No. 1 up to No. 12. The broad pencil in size from $\frac{1}{8}$ of an inch upward is used for stripes of any size above $\frac{1}{8}$ of an inch in width; but the round fine lining pencils have been generally superseded by what is known as the "sword pencil," or "dagger pencil." These are not generally for sale in the stores.

and the painter must make them to suit his wants. To do this, take a piece of hickory or other strong wood and cut the handle as shown in the accompanying engraving, Fig. 9. The flattened part is that held between the thumb and finger. Next split the end, and put a pin across the split to keep it open; then take from a large pencil a small bunch of hair, say fifty hairs, and dipping the butt end in melted glue, lay them carefully in the split, draw out the pin, when the parts will close together, and then a piece of thread may be tied around over the split to secure it. The ends of the hairs should not be cut if it can by any means be avoided, as the

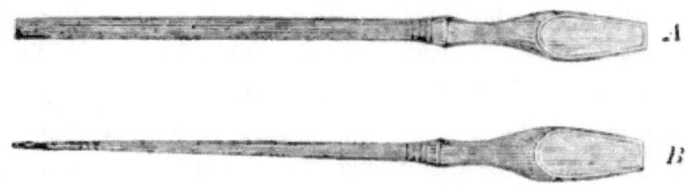

Fig. 9.—"*Dagger*" *Pencils.*

cutting tends to destroy the softness of the point. In our illustration *A* is a "dagger pencil" when dry, and *B* is the same when wet with paint.

These pencils are held *edgewise* to the work, and but one-half the length of hair is allowed to touch the surface. A stripe from five to six feet in length may be drawn without refilling the pencil, the large quantity of hair acting as a reservoir for the paint; and several sizes of lines may be made with the same pencil by simply regulating the pressure upon it, a heavy pressure making a heavy stripe and a light one a finer stripe. The painter may easily learn to do this by practice, although beginners may find it difficult to maintain a uniform pressure, and consequently a uniform stripe over all parts of the work.

The hair for striping pencils should be at least two and a quarter inches long—if too long the hairs will droop or sag down, and if too short, a straight line cannot be made.

Ox-hair pencils, also used in striping, are made from the hair which grows in the ear of the animal, and these are considered excellent for striping wagon gears, particularly where heavy color is used.

Fig. 10 represents the striping pencils used by New York painters.

Fig. 10.—Striping Pencils.

The proper position of the hand while striping the rim of a wheel is shown in Fig. 11. The pencil is held between the thumb and fore-finger and the other fingers act as a gauge or guide. During the striping, the wheel is kept revolving by the left hand, while the pencil is held stationary in the right hand. The pencil will require refilling frequently, and care should be taken that this is done uniformly.

ZINC PALETTES.

A zinc palette is said to be the best for working or thinning the paint upon, as it is so easily cleaned after its use. Procure a piece of smooth zinc say three inches wide and nine inches long, cut the ends round, and make a hole in one end by which to hang it up when not in use. The pencil is first dipped into the paint and then worked out to make it uniform upon the zinc palette. To extend a stripe where the paint has been insufficient in the first movement, the line should be retraced for several inches, or the connecting stripe will be smaller or not so well covered as other parts.

Small tin cups are best for holding the striping paint—blacking boxes or lids to tin boxes may be used to advan-

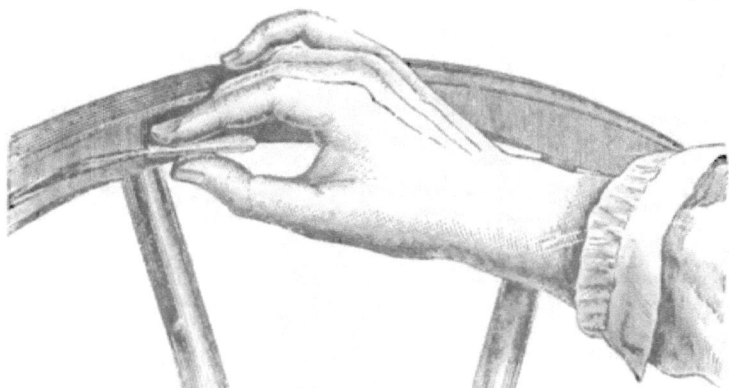

Fig. 11.—Showing the Position of the Hand in Striping the Rim of a Wheel.

tage—many use large clam-shells, and we believe it a good plan, as when they are gummed up with old paint they can be thrown away with no loss.

CARE OF PENCILS.

Pencils should be well cared for after use. It is a good plan to keep them in a small wooden box with a lid to exclude dust, and supplied with a piece of glass upon the bottom on which to spread the pencils. They should be well rinsed in turpentine after use, then greased with a mixture of tallow and sweet oil—which does not harden in cold weather—and nicely straightened out and stuck fast to the glass, the broad ones on one side and grading the sizes down to the hair liners, so that in case one is missing from its place it can readily be discovered, and so that any particular size can be taken up without disturbing the others. When a pencil gets bent or crooked, grease it and draw the hairs between the finger and a warm iron.

PENCILS FOR ORNAMENTAL STRIPING.

The pencils for ornamental striping are similar to those spoken of, but the hairs are shorter, and a long wooden handle is necessary. The hair should be about half an inch in length, and we have always given preference to red sable hair. In case these pencils cannot be easily procured, a camel's-hair striper may be cut down and drawn through a fine quill.

COLORS FOR STRIPING.

The paint or "striping color" may be mixed as for color on bodies, but it may be found best with some colors to add a little more oil. Tube colors are preferred by some, but we do not agree with the plan of using them for striping, from the fact that they are all "too short," *i. e.,* do not *flow* as nicely from the pencil as home-made colors do. A smart rub with the stone and muller will render any of the ordinary pigments fine enough.

CHAPTER VII.

WAGON STRIPING.

Carriage striping and wagon striping are two distinct branches of trade, and yet he who can do the one well will be equally successful in the other, by which we mean, it is not the manipulation of the tools which distinguishes one from the other, but the *style*, the position of the stripes, and the colors. Therefore, when once the carriage striper learns where and *how to place* his stripes on a

Fig. 12. Showing a Striping generally used on Business Wagon Gears.

wagon he becomes a wagon striper, and *vice versa*. The carriage striper has certain arbitrary combinations of striping, each having a name, as for example the following:

" Hair line."

" Fine line."

" Medium."

"Stout line."

"Round line."

"Heavy round line."

"Light stripe."

"Narrow stripe."

"Medium stripe."

"Heavy stripe."

"Broad stripe."

"Double fine line."

"Double medium line."

"Double stout line."

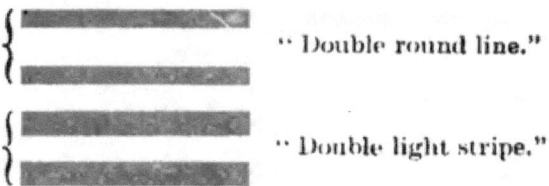
"Double round line."

"Double light stripe."

But these are ignored by the wagon striper, most of his work being that known as "panel striping" on gears and fine lining on bodies.

The stripes generally put upon business-wagon gears are a three-sixteenth of an inch stripe and a fine line, as shown in fig. 12.

These stripes are sometimes put on plain and sometimes twisted in various forms to give variety or to "fill up" certain parts as shown in Figs. 13 and 14.

All such work is done off-hand—that is, no pattern is used, the eye alone guiding the hand, and it is surprising, sometimes, to see the uniformity given to wagon stripes, when it is remembered that not even a mark was made to insure it. There is as much necessity for practice in laying out the striping as there is in making the stripe, and we frequently see apprentice boys devoting all their spare time in practice at such work.

In Fig. 15 is shown a panel stripe for spring bar and like pieces, the fine line being generally "put in" in two colors, as for example, if the fine line be white on a dark ground, the feathering and dots may be "put in" with light blue or red. A few light touches with the striping pencil will often add to the appearance of a job, and these should never be begrudged.

Fig. 16 shows the manner of striping the top of a spring, the broad stripe being run on the edge of the leaves, and

THE COMPLETE CARRIAGE AND WAGON PAINTER. 59

a simple straight fine line finishing it. This part of the gear is not so easily seen as the other parts, and it would

Fig. 13. Striping for Business Wagon Gears. Fig. 14.—Another Method of Striping Gears.

60   THE COMPLETE CARRIAGE AND WAGON PAINTER.

be a waste of time to elaborate the striping; however, if other parts are profusely covered with fine lines, these places should at least approximate thereto.

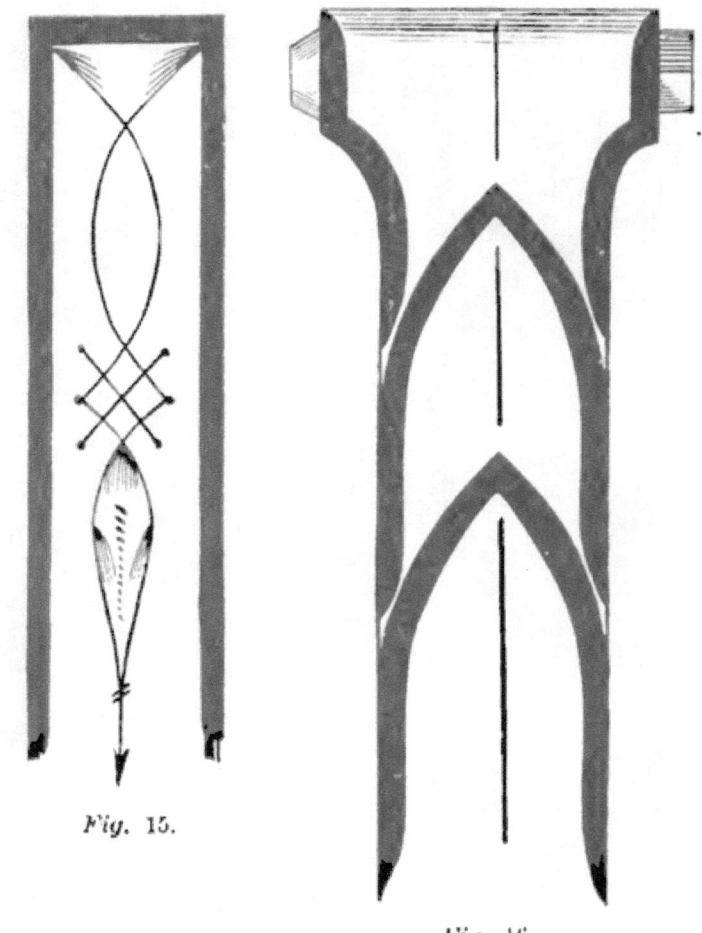

Fig. 15. Panel Striping for Spring-bars.   Fig. 16. Striping the Top of a Spring.

Fig. 17 shows the back end of the shafts, and a portion of the cross-bar, giving an idea how a stripe may be put on such places.

Fig. 17. Showing a method of Striping the Cross-bar and back end of the Shaft.

BREAKING LINES.

Fig. 18 illustrates what is known as a "break" in a "double fine line," and is used to break the monotony of a continuous stripe. It is useful on body bolts or name panels as well as on gears.

A "POUNCE BAG."

Fig. 19 gives a general idea of the finish at the end of a panel stripe. Such designs require patterns, and to make them, take a piece of thin tissue paper and copy the illustration, or draw a new design, then perforate the paper with a needle into small holes, thus:

. . . .

following every outline of the design; then tie up in a piece of thin muslin some whiting to form a "pounce-bag." Lay the paper pattern upon the desired spot, holding it firmly, or fasten it with tacks, and rub or pounce the whiting from the bag over it. The whiting will penetrate the holes and leave a well-defined outline on the work, which may be followed with the pencil and paint.

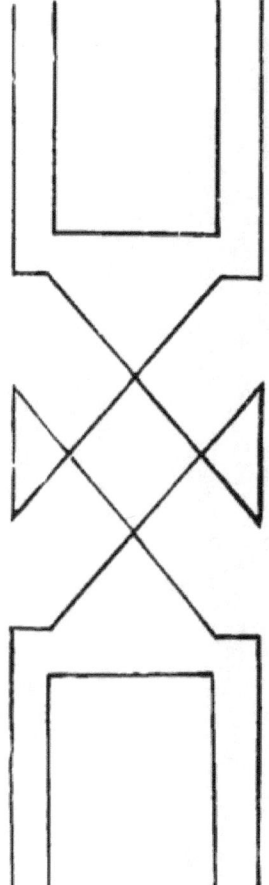

Fig. 18, Showing a "Break" in Striping.

Fig. 20 is a similar design. These come under the head of flat scrolling, of which more anon.

It is the usual plan with ribbed bodies to "black off" the ribs on all work painted in dark colors, such as green, blue, brown, etc., but where the job is light, as vermilion, Paris green, cream or yellow, the contrast would be too great, and therefore the ribs are striped on the chamfers

Fig. 19.—*Showing a Finish for the End of a Panel Stripe.*

Fig. 20.—*Showing another Style of Finish for the end of a Panel Stripe.*

with a $\frac{3}{16}$-inch stripe of black, thus "lightening up" the appearance of the job.

Ornamental corners are frequently added, and particularly where the panels are striped; but striping on the panels of a ribbed job is very seldom seen, and then on cheap work only.

GOLD STRIPING.

Gold striping is done in the following manner: First, having the body well rubbed out of color-and-varnish with pulverized pumice stone and washed clean, it is necessary to pounce over the entire panel on which the striping is to go, with the whiting pounce-bag. This leaves a thin film of the powder on the surface and prevents the gold leaf from sticking to any part not covered with gilding size.*

GILDING SIZE.

The size used for this work may be a mixture of one part finishing varnish and two parts good brown japan.

The proportions may be changed to suit the time at disposal, but the formula given will make a size which will set "tacky" in an hour, in good weather. A very little turpentine may be used to thin the size upon the palette, and care must be taken that the size is not "fat," leaving heavy edges to the stripe.

The size should flow down smooth and even in all parts, and the gold leaf should not be laid on until the hand can be gently passed over it without sticking—but when placed directly upon it the size appears "tacky" or "sticky."

When the gilding size is too "wet," the gilding will be rough; and when too "dry," the gold leaf will not adhere

---

* We use the word "*gilding* size" to distinguish it from a *drier* or sort of japan found in the market under the name of "gold-size," which is not intended, nor can it be used for laying gold upon. Many are led astray by the name, and the anathemas heaped upon it when put to use as a gilding size are often heavy enough to sink it to oblivion—where it ought to be.

to it, so it is of the utmost importance that the size be in proper condition. Gold leaf is purchased in small books of 25 leaves, 3½ inches square, the price ranging from 30 to 50 cents per book. There are three grades, viz.: light, medium and deep; the latter generally receiving the preference.

APPLYING GOLD LEAF.

There are several ways of applying the leaf to the stripe, but the tools used by the frame gilder such as "tip" "cushion," "gold knife," etc., should find no resting place in the wagon shop; there is no need of them except when working on glass or in gilding scrolls and figures carved in wood for circus or band chariots, *then* those tools may be employed. When about to lay a gold leaf on striping first cut the back of the book with a sharp knife, or with a pair of shears, so that each leaf is separate, then lift the first leaf and laying it on a flat surface rub it gently with a piece of white wax or better still, a piece of paraffine candle. This slightly greases the paper and if it be replaced upon the gold the leaf will adhere very closely to it. Next lift and grease the second, and so on until the whole 25 leaves are done; then with a sharp knife, guided by a straight-edge, cut through the book, making strips a trifle wider than the stripe; the gold will then adhere nicely to the paper and no great care need be taken in handling it.

Now, the gilding size being " tacky," lift one of the strips of paper and gold and carefully place the gold upon the size; gently rub the finger over the back or paper, then take the paper away and the gold will be found nicely fastened upon the gilding size; go on with the next until the size is covered, take up any loose gold with the tip of the finger, and repair any broken or missed places; then wipe over gently with a bunch of soft cotton.

Another plan is to dampen the paper with turpentine instead of using wax or paraffine, but we do not believe it so good a plan as the one just described.

GOLD STRIPING.

A gilding machine, invented by George W. Langdon, of Baraboo, Wis., answers a very good purpose where much gold striping is done. It consists of various sized wheels, having rubber rims, fitted to an adjustable handle, and so arranged that the wheels may be readily changed for any width of stripe. To use it, the leaf is laid upon a leather cushion and cut, as when using a "tip" in frame gilding. The wheel is now rolled over the cut piece, which adheres to the rubber tire, and then, if the wheel be rolled in like manner over the size, the gold will leave the rubber and adhere to the size. One single straightforward motion will distribute the leaf upon a tacky surface or stripe, leaving nine inches of gold stripe perfectly laid. Many lay the leaf directly from the book, rolling it over the gilding size as desired; but this must be left for experts, as an amateur would waste a large share of gold thereby.

When the striping is finished and quite dry, the job should be washed with soap and water to remove any greasiness or paraffine, which would cause trouble with the varnish; then it will generally be found best to run a fine line of white, blue, red or green on the edge of the gold to straighten out any defects. A red fine line on one edge and a cream-colored fine line on the other will look well on green grounds.

Gold bronze is used extensively for gilding wagon work, and if a good quality of bronze be purchased some excellent work may be done with it. The preparation of the surface, and the size used, are the same as for gold leaf, the only difference being that bronze is a fine powder instead of leaf. To apply the bronze take a piece of shammy, velvet or plush and tie it up into a small pad, then dipping it into the bronze gently rub it over the work. It is a good plan to coat the stripe of bronze over with French shellac varnish before laying on copal varnish, for there is something like an acid in ordinary varnish, particularly English varnish, which acts on the bronze and bringing a sort of verdigris to the surface causes the gold to darken. The shellac prevents this.

"GOLD PAINT."

There is what is called "gold paint" in market, which is extensively used for striping, but it is simply gold bronze mixed with a thin japan, and, as any one can make it for himself, it should be left to school-boys and artistically inclined females. Silver leaf and silver bronze are seldom used, owing to their liability to change color and become almost dark; but a substitute can now be found in dealers' stores which does not turn color, and it is extensively used on street cars. Nickel leaf is the name of this substitute; it comes in tissue paper book, 4½ inches square. "Dutch metal" is only fit for scene-painters' use. There are also various colored bronzes, but as they are seldom used on wagon work, we will pass them by.

CHAPTER VIII.

COLORS EMPLOYED ON WAGONS.

No. 1. *Rib Body Business Wagon.*—Body, chrome green or milori green; ribs and frame, black, striped with fine lines of white, cream color, or vermilion; gears, cream color, striped with broad lines, from $\frac{3}{16}$ to $\frac{1}{4}$ inch wide, of blue, dark green, or black, and fine lines of vermilion or blue.

No. 2. *Same Style of Wagon.*—Body, Indian red glazed with carmine; black frame, striped with vermilion or cream color; gears, light English vermilion, striped as above with black, and white fine lines.

No. 3. *Same.*—Body, medium chrome yellow; ribs striped as before directed (not "blacked off"), fine lines of red or black; gears, light English vermilion, striped $\frac{3}{16}$ in. black, and fine lines of white.

No. 4.—Body, deep English vermilion; ribs striped black, and fine lines of white; gears, light vermilion, striped black and white.

No. 5. *Delivery Wagon.*—Body panels, deep carmine; belt panel, dark green; top, black; gears, dark green, striped with double fine line of gold, either leaf or bronze.

No. 6. *Same.*—Body panels, deep olive green; belt panel, carmine; top, black; lettering, gold; gears, light vermilion glazed with carmine, striped with black and fine line of gold.

No. 7. *Same.*—Body panels, black; moldings, carmine; belt, light olive green; top sides, deep carmine; all the rest black; gears, dark olive green, with black and cream fine lines.

PAINTING A WHITE JOB.

It is a well known fact that white jobs, such as circus wagons, sleighs, hearses, etc., will remain white and wear better if the surface be polished or rubbed to an egg-shell gloss instead of receiving a coat of clear varnish. To do such work, bring up the foundation as before directed, except that in using *lead color,* pure white lead be substituted, and *white rough-stuff* also takes the place of the slate-colored or dark variety. To make such rough-stuff, take dry white lead, one part; pulverized soapstone, two parts; ground pumice stone, one part; and mix with brown japan and turpentine; then add a gill of oil to each pint of paint.

When the job is rubbed out of rough-stuff apply two coats of pure white lead as color, follow this with color and varnish made of keg lead one part, zinc white one part and grind in rubbing varnish. When that is dry and has been nicely rubbed with pulverized pumice stone, apply a second coat of color and varnish made in the same manner, but substituting wearing body varnish for the rubbing. When this coat is dry give the work a gentle rub with pumice stone and water until a nice egg-shell appearance is obtained, wash off, and put on the striping, lettering or whatever it is, and then pencil-varnish the stripes or letters, leaving the white ground untouched. This will give a beautiful white, and a better job than any other method we have yet discovered.

CHAPTER IX.

WAGON LETTERING.

In these days of great inventions, when we can purchase "lettering ready made," in pasteboard patterns nicely cut out, templets of metal, whereby the whole alphabet may be marked out, and finally ingeniously contrived transfers or decalcomania, it seems almost a waste of time to lay out directions for painting letters with a pencil. But our plan would be incomplete without a chapter on the laying out and painting of letters for wagons and cars. It was at one time the wagon letterers' good fortune to possess "an occupation and a name" above that of the sign writer. His work could be readily distinguished from the ordinary letterer or sign painter by its boldness and the care given to details, particularly in shading, where glazings of carmine or other transparent pigments gave a richness and finish which could not emanate from the hands of those not intimately connected with the trade. These days have gone by, and we find the well known and approved style of the wagon letterer prostituted to the idiosyncrasies of house and sign painters, who have migrated, some from foreign shores, others from their regular trade, to swell the ranks as professionals (?) in wagon shops. The consequence is, that instead of having a few standard styles of letters to write about, we might, to cover the subject, take our text from a printer's specimen book, so varied and multitudinous are the letters now in vogue.

The aim of the wagon letterer should be to make his work plain, yet bold and attractive, for the words he puts upon a wagon are to be read as the vehicle is in motion, while he who wishes to decipher a sign may pause in his walk to do so. Therefore, fine lines, as in some of the Roman letters, and all fancifully-twisted arabesques, called letters, are out of place on the sides of a wagon.

The standard styles of the wagon letterer are the FULL BLOCK, round and octagon; HALF BLOCK, round and octagon; SOLID BLOCK and ITALIC; and these, extended or condensed.

Fig. 21.—Octagon Full Block Letters.

The *Full Block* letter partakes much of the character of the Roman letter. It is bold, or "heavy on the face," and when well made is by far the handsomest one on the list. This style of letter never looks well condensed, but it may be extended to an almost unlimited extent, without the loss of any of its characteristics. In its normal condition the Full Block occupies nearly a square space (see **Fig**

21), the measurement always being taken from the outer edge of the main bars, the "spurs" being allowed to run over at will. There are but few letters of the alphabet which fill the same space, and when an attempt is made

Fig. 22.—*The Full Block Round Letter.*

to form the letters geometrically, a mechanical rather than an artistic appearance is given.

An octagon Full Block letter possesses a geometrical equilibrium superior to the *Round Letter*, but the latter (Fig. 22)

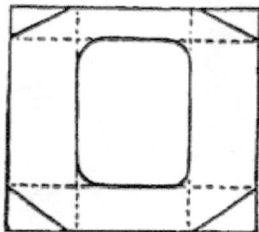

Fig. 23.—*Showing the Method of Cutting off the Corners of Round Letters.*

is frequently used on good work to give variety. These letters are generally made with the lower spurs a trifle heavier than the upper ones, and this is done to give a more solid foundation, although the difference is almost imperceptible—and the eye is deceived as it is when looking at the letter S, which is much larger in its lower circle than the upper one—(see S right, and S wrong side up). The corners are cut off at an angle a very little less than the width of the bars of the letter, (see Fig. 23), although in the extended letter, (Fig. 24) the corners may be cut off from line to line.

The Round Full Block, as before said, may be used to

Fig. 24.—Showing how the Corners are Cut off Extended Letters.

give variety, but it is not so neat a letter as the octagon. In all respects this letter is the same as the octagon except in the formation of the corners.

The Half Block letter is next in order. This letter is simply the "gothic" of the printer, with a few alterations. We show in Fig. 25 the octagon half block, which is one of the most useful letters of the wagon painter. It may be condensed, but its extension is not advised beyond a small limit. Fig. 26 shows the half block round letter. There are some peculiarities about the half block style of letter that we wish to call particular attention to. First, the formation of the

74   THE COMPLETE CARRIAGE AND WAGON PAINTER.

letter M. We show in Figs. 27, 28 and 29 the difference made by letterers. Fig. 27 being the recognized or correct

Fig. 25.—Octagon Half Block Letters.

Fig. 26.—Half Block Round Letters.

one. Again in Figs. 30, 31 and 32 the letter R, round half

block, is shown in three styles, some preferring 80, others 31, while 32 is a showcard writer's letter.

Fig. 27.—*Showing the Correct Method of forming the Half Block Letter M.*

Fig. 28.   Fig. 29.

Showing two Incorrect Methods of forming the Half Block Letter M.

The letter G has its crossbar carried across as shown in

Fig. 30.   Fig. 31.   Fig. 32.

Showing the Letter R in Three Styles.

Fig. 33, which is a sign writer's style, the true wagon letter G being formed as shown in Fig. 34. The outline letter

Fig. 33.—*A Show Card Letter G.*

Fig. 34.—*The Letter G as Correctly Formed by Wagon Letterers*

is simply a letter outlined and not filled in. It is extensively used on the sunk bottoms of street cars and omni-

Fig. 35.—*The Outline Letter.*

buses, but seldom seen in other places.
Fig. 35 is an illustration of this style of letter.

The *square block letter* is made with all its parts alike in width, or nearly so. We show in Fig. 36 the *solid block*

LACQUE

Fig. 36.—*Solid Block Letters.*

letter, and this may be made either octagon or round. It is a very bold letter, borrowed from the type-founder who

Fig. 37.—*Italic Letters.*

calls it "Antique." When nicely shaded it is very handsome, and is extensively used in New York. *Italic letters*

HINE

Fig. 38.—*Another Style of Italic Letters.*

are simply letters set at an angle, as shown in Figs. 37 and 38.

The *printer's black letter*, generally called by the letterer

Fig. 39.—*Printer's Black Letter or German Text.*

LONDON

Fig. 40.—Ornamental Letters.

"*German text*," we show in Fig. 39. This letter makes a very tasteful line, if well put on, and may often be seen

PICKED

Fig. 41.—Another Style of Ornamental Letters.

on the delivery wagons of *bon ton* storekeepers.

Ornamental letters, as shown in Figs. 40 and 41, look well on some jobs; being *bold*, they are much better

LEVERS

Fig. 42.—The Tuscan Full Block Letter.

adapted for wagons than the Roman and many others now used.

The *Tuscan full-block* letter, shown in Fig. 42, may be used in place of the ordinary full-block, and particularly where a condensed letter is desired.

THE COMPLETE CARRIAGE AND WAGON PAINTER.   79

It is a singular fact that almost every particular city has a local style of lettering, both for wagons and signs. Bos-

Fig. 43.

Fig. 44.

Fig. 45.

Three Styles of Letters used by the Abbot Downing Co.

ton has a very peculiar style; Philadelphia another; yet they all appear well when one gets accustomed to them.

The Abbot Downing Co., of Concord, N. H., introduced a new and tasteful style of lettering for express wagons, which we show in Figs. 43, 44, 45.

CHAPTER X.

WAGON LETTERING CONTINUED.

THE ROMAN LETTER.

The Roman letter may be taken as the standard or base for all other alphabets. It is used more extensively now than in former years on every description of work, but it is seldom we see a perfectly formed letter, owing in a great degree to carelessness on the part of the student when learning its peculiarities. The graceful turn of the letter S, the

Fig. 46.—The Modern Old Style Letter.

lower limb of the letter R, or the short and (&) seem to be something that few can master, and for that reason a sort of hybrid letter has of late been introduced, in which the difficult parts may be said to be avoided. We show in Fig. 46 the letters R and E, to illustrate the points spoken of. As will be seen, the letter R is provided with a straight limb or tail, and the E possesses features which take away the uniformity or squareness of the letter, and thus the necessity of reaching a high standard of Roman lettering is obviated, and the workman is enabled to palm off an abortion and call it perfection. This style of letter is called " modern old style," and its introduction may be laid directly to the influx of second-rate workmen.

There is a marked difference in the formation of the Roman letter in different cities. To clearly show this, we present the New York Roman letter in comparison with the Boston Roman, the former being considered by the general public as the most graceful in outline and correct in principles. These letters were painted in black and then photo-engraved to the size here shown (Fig. 47) for this work.

Fig. 47.—The New York Roman Letter.

Fig. 47.—*Continued.*

Fig. 47.—Continued.

Fig. 47.—*Continued.*

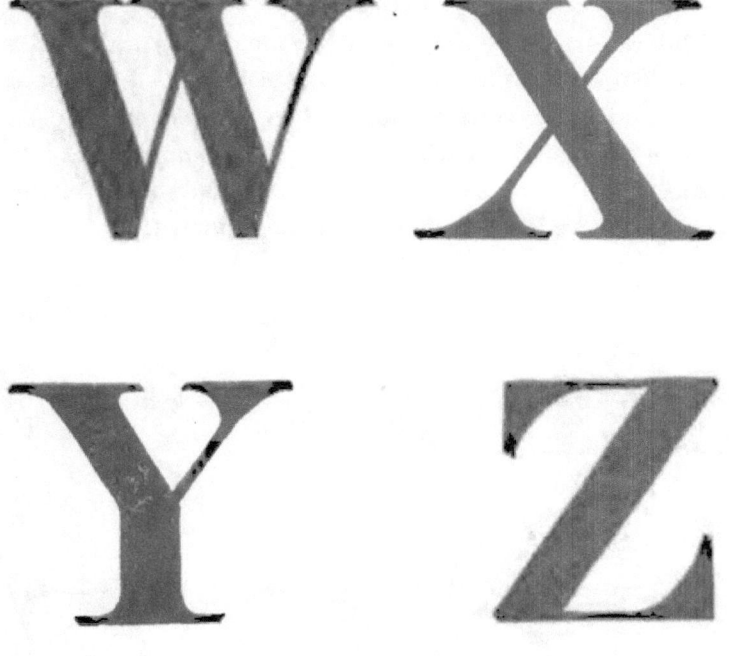

Fig. 47.—Continued.

THE NEW YORK ROMAN ITALIC.

This letter is one quite easily made, after a thorough knowledge of the Roman letter has been gained, for it is very similar in construction. It is extensively used on wagon sides to give variety to the work, and it certainly looks well, if care is taken to make the slants of each letter correctly. In Fig. 48 we present the alphabet.

Fig. 48.—The New York Roman Italic Letter.

J K L

M N O

P Q R

S T U

Fig. 48.—*Continued.*

Fig. 48.—*Continued.*

The "*Lower Case*" letters are shown in Fig. 49.

Fig. 49.—*New York Roman Italic, Lower Case.*

lmnop

qrstuv

wxyz

Fig. 49.—Continued.

THE BOSTON ROMAN

This style, as shown in Fig. 50, is the outgrowth of the work of artists of this country and of Europe from century to century. The crude characters at the beginning, no doubt, would not for a moment bear comparison with those used at the present time. The letters combine the boldness of the block with the grace and symmetry of the script, and are preferred by the business men of Boston to any other style of letter made, although the Queen Anne **revivalists have played sad havoc with their pet hobby.**

Fig. 50.—*The Boston Roman Letter.*

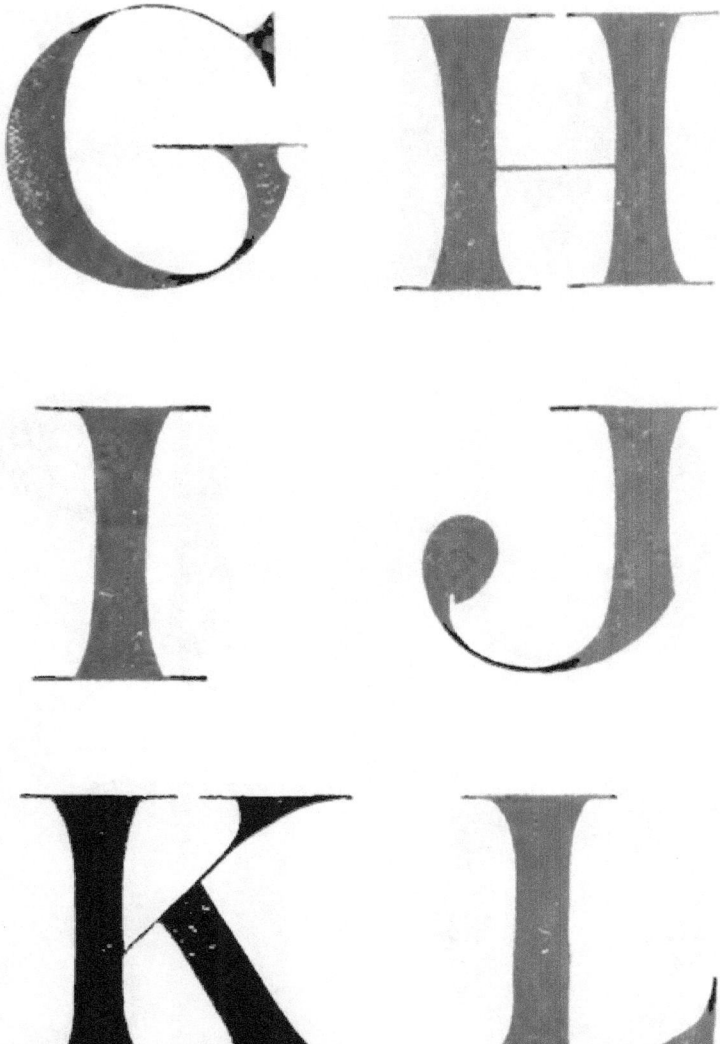

Fig. 50.—Continued.

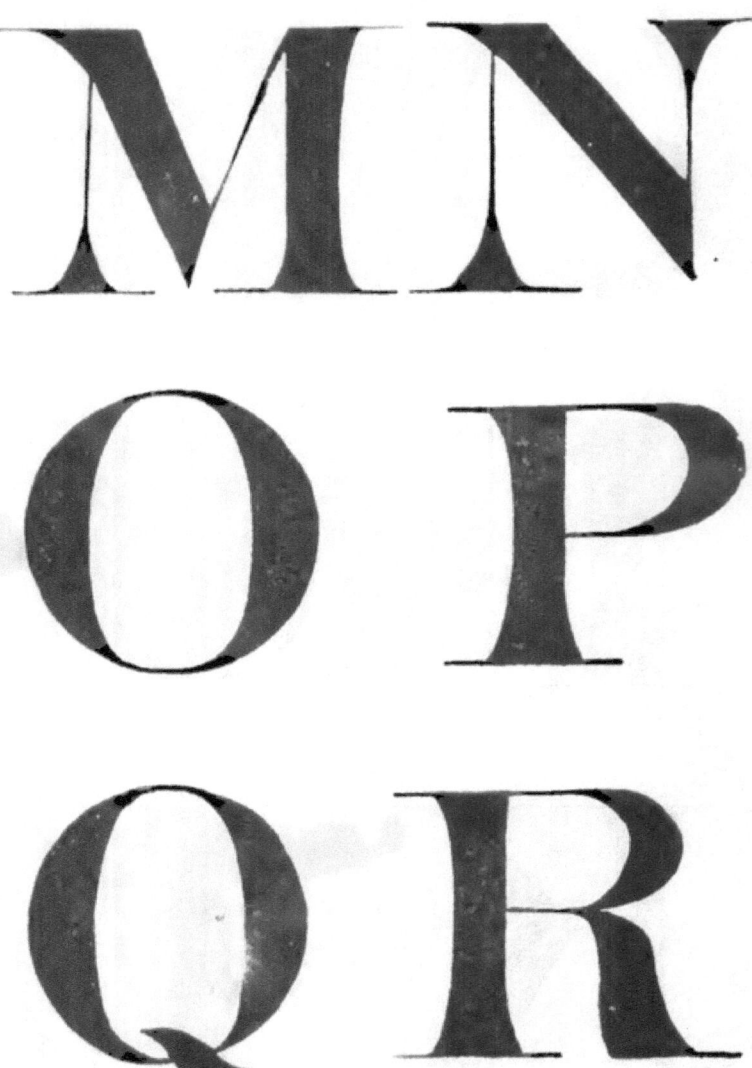

Fig. 50.—Continued.

Fig. 50.—Continued.

Fig. 50.—*Continued.*

Among a dozen first-class sign writers there is considerable difference in opinion and custom as to minor points in the construction and spacing in this alphabet, especially the letters B, C, P, R and S, and letters involving like curves and principles. When used on wagon, car or sign work, it looks best in gold on a black smalt ground.

In this letter, each, with a few exceptions, occupies a square. The letters C, G, O and Q are described within a perfect circle, although the minor curves must be drawn free-hand, observing to keep the proper thickness, which is a trifle more in these letters than in the heavy perpendiculars of most other letters. The thickness, according to the best authorities should be two-ninths of the height, although the appearance is good when made one-fifth. The hair lines extend right and left from the grace lines two-thirds of the two-ninths, and the grace equal in width to the hair line.

Observe, however, that the hair and grace lines are a trifle shorter above the centre of the letter, and should be made one-sixteenth of two-ninths the thickness. Also notice that the lower arms of the B, E, S and Z are a trifle longer and heavier than the upper ones, which serves to balance the letters, otherwise they would appear top-heavy. Avoid spacing this letter too openly, as that gives a scattered appearance.

CHAPTER XI.

LAYING OUT WORK.

In laying out work first prepare the surface, if for gold letters, by pouncing the panel with whiting, dust off nicely, then draw the lines which form the boundary of the letter with chalk.

Taking the most useful letter for either wagons or cars, and one quite easily made, for a criterion, i. e., the HALF-

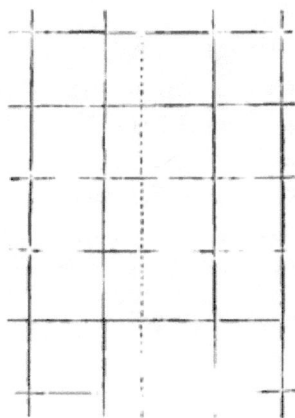

Fig. 51.—Showing how a Half Block Letter is Designed.

BLOCK LETTER, we proceed as shown in Fig. 51, by first laying out the top and bottom lines, then divide the space between them into five spaces, for a perfectly formed letter is one-fifth higher than wide. By this plan you will make six horizontal lines. The bars of a letter of this kind should be equal to one-fifth its height, consequently, we now have the lines for the top bar, the bottom bar, and the middle bar of the letter. We next divide the horizontal lines by perpendicular ones, forming three and a half squares, and this gives us the extreme dimensions of the octagon block B, C, D, G, H, O, P, Q, R, S, T, U, V, Z, &. The

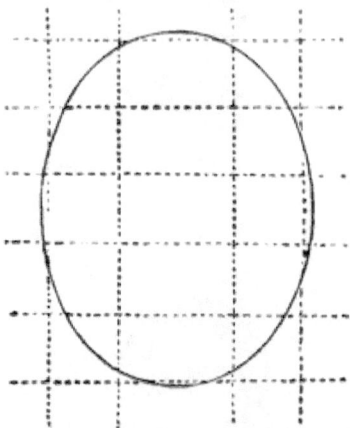

Fig. 52.—*Showing how an Ellipse is Used in Making Round Letters.*

round block letters occupy a very little more space, say, one-quarter of a square, the letters E, F, J, N and L being one-quarter of a square less than the extreme boundary. The letter I is simply the width of one square. The letter W extends over one square, making it occupy four and one-half squares.

In Fig. 52 we show how the ellipse is used in making round letters. All round letters are governed in their circular parts by the ellipse, or oval as it is more frequently called, and to illustrate this fact we present here in Fig. 53 the alphabet in lower case letters of the Gothic Half Block style.

Fig. 53.—Gothic Half Block Letter, Lower Case.

j k l

m n o

p q r

Fig. 53.—Continued.

s t u

v w x

y z

Fig. 58.—Continued.

To make an ellipse will now occupy our attention.

Supposing the line of letters we are about to form are five inches high, we must, in order to have the line appear perfectly straight, or the letters of one height, make all the round letters, *i. e.*, C, G, O, S, Q, to extend a trifle above and below the lines, say one-eighth of an inch, as illustrated in Fig. 52, otherwise these letters would appear smaller than the others in the line. To lay out such

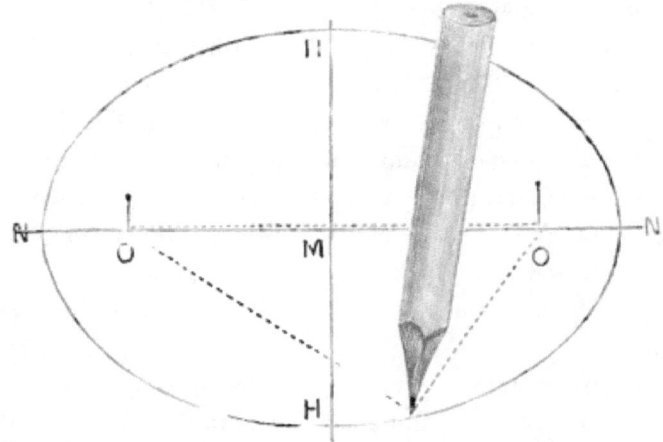

Fig. 54.—Showing the Manner of Drawing the Ellipse.

letters then, using an ellipse, we cut from a card a pattern after it has been drawn in the following manner: The oval or ellipse must be a very little over five inches long, and a very little over three and a half inches wide. First draw a horizontal line through the centre, which will be seen in the engraving, Fig. 54, marked *N N*. Then across its centre draw a vertical line *H H*. Next measure from the centre one-half the desired length of the ellipse, *i. e.*, two and three-quarter inches each way or line *N*, and one and three-quarter inches on line *H*, which gives the space that the oval or ellipse must fill. Now take the compasses (or dividers) and putting one leg on the centre *M* place the other leg at the point, two and three-quarter inches off on line *N*, lift the compasses, being careful not to displace them, and set one leg on spot *H*, one and three-quarter inches from centre, and turn the other leg down to line *N*, which it will strike a short distance inside of the spot *N*, and that spot is marked *O* in the engraving. Then turn it to the other side of centre *M*, and mark the other spot *O* on line *N*. Now stick a pin or tack into the spots *O O* and *H*, and tie a piece of thread around the three pins. Next, remove the pin at *H*, and put in its place a pencil, as shown in the engraving, and, keeping the thread taut, move the pencil along. You will find that the string directs the course of the pencil point, and the result will be a perfectly-drawn ellipse.

The ellipse may be made any size or shape, *i. e.*, long and narrow, or broad and short, by simply laying out the measurements on the lines *H* and *N*. For instance, if we measure twenty inches on the line *N* and four inches on the line *H* the ellipse will be long and slim, but nevertheless a a perfect ellipse. Having drawn the ellipse, lay the card upon a piece of glass, and with a sharp knife, cut out the pattern, which may then be used for marking out the round letters C, G, D, O, Q, S, and the lower part of the letters U and J.

The card-board ellipse is laid upon the proper place, and the pencil is passed around it, then the points as in C and

G are formed. The lower end of the letter G, i. e., its cross-bar, is made a very little lower than the middle bar lines.

A small ellipse pattern for laying out the lower case of the alphabet, shown in Fig. 53, will be found excellent, for nearly all of these letters are based upon the oval. The lower case letters are made 3½ squares of the capitals in

Fig. 55.—*Showing Four Properly Balanced Figures.*

height, and the long letters such as b, d, f, h, k and l, run up to the full five squares, while g j, p, q, and y run below an equal distance, making either letter five squares in height.

All letters should have a perfect balance, that is, if they were cut out of a block they could be set upon their bases. We here illustrate a few figures to show this feature (see Fig. 55) as well as to illustrate three of the most difficult figures to make, so that they will be evenly balanced, namely, 5, 3 and 2.

CHAPTER XII.

SHADING.

Again we are called upon to deplore the inroads made by sign and show card letterers. It was formerly the custom to shade all letters on the *right side and bottom*, except in the case of the sunk-bottom of cars, when the shade was thrown on the *top* and *right* side. But now we see the shade frequently put upon the *left* of the letter (it is easier to do, they say), which entirely breaks the charac-

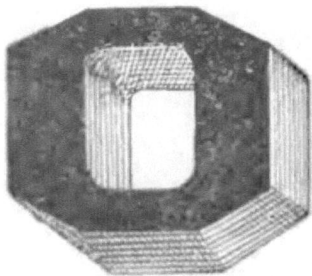

Fig. 56.—Showing an Octagon Half Block with a Single Shade Blocked.

teristic of the wagon letterer. There may be a few sign writers who can letter a wagon according to rule, but, as a general thing, their work falls below the standard.

We show in Fig. 56 an octagon half-block with a *single shade, blocked, i, e.,* made darker on the bottom than on the sides. This may be done by shading with vermilion on the sides and ends, then glazing the bottom with carmine. Fig. 57 shows a *double shade blocked*. This may be done by shading the sides vermilion, the bottom Indian red, and then running on the second shade over each, covering one-half the width with carmine. It should be remembered that the *darkest* shade *always* comes nearest the letter. On gold lettering the shade always touches the edge of the gold, but in paint letters a space is left between the letter and shade, see Fig. 58. The shade never looks well if made wider than the bars of the letter, and the angles formed by the end of the shade should be uniform, and should be determined by the angle of the square—generally forty-five degrees. However, the shade is sometimes made wider on the bottom than on the sides, and then the angle will be inclined more nearly to a perpendicular.

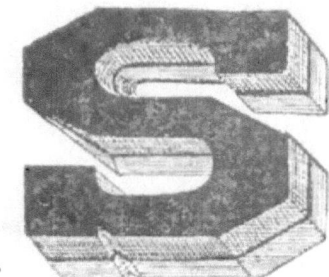

Fig. 57.—*Showing a Double Shade Blocked.*

Shading should be done in the same manner throughout a piece of work; that is, if one line be shaded on the right side, all lines on the job must be done so. On red grounds, gold letters are generally shaded with black, and then the double shade is made by extending the width of the shade, by running a carmine glaze outside of the black. The colors employed in shading should harmonize with the colors of the letter and of the groundwork. Here the taste of the painter is called into play, for if the colors are not harmonious—no matter how well formed the letters may be—the result will not be satisfactory.

Gold letters on a white ground may be shaded with any colors excepting those of a yellow hue—blue, red and green being the colors most frequently used.

Red letters look well shaded with lead color or gray; a

Fig. 58.—Showing the Method of Shading "Painted" Letters.

light green will also be a complementary shade for red, on a white ground. Black letters look well shaded with any of the primary colors. One thing should ever be taken into consideration, *the most intense or prominent color should be put on the letter, and not the shade.* When a shade has been put on a letter, and a disagreeable result is produced, it may often be improved by adding a fine line of white or black (according to the ground) between the shade and letter. All gold lettering should be edged—

called "*the lights*"—on the opposite edge from the shade, or in some cases all around the letter. The *cast shadow* of a letter is in reality the *shade*, and what is generally called the shade is the "thickness" or "blocking." This cast shadow is seldom added except on white grounds, when a faint lead color or French gray is used.

The position of lines should receive attention. It will not look well to have two circular lines follow one another. Curved lines—as the line of beauty—are often thrown in to relieve the appearance of sameness. All short or unimportant words, such as "and,' "dealer in," "in," "manufacturer of," etc., should be placed alone, or worked into a ribbon or scroll, and *never* attached to the end of a long line of greater importance.

The same style of letter should not be employed in two adjacent lines, except it be in the enumeration of a list of articles, or several addresses. Letters belonging to different classes or styles should not be used in the same line, except it be for ornamental purposes, and then they should be used sparingly.

The tools used by the letterer may be counted upon the fingers. The pallette and rest-stick are so well known they need no description, and then there are the straightedge, rule, compasses, chalk and a piece of string. The pencils should be of black sable-hair, either in quills or tin. The hair should be about one inch long. The pencil, when dipped in turpentine or paint, should present a fine point, and when spread upon the work should assume a square or flat end, that corners may be easily formed.

Camel's hair pencils answer a very good purpose, but are

not so good as a well "broke in" sable. Fine liners may be made by cutting the hair from a large pencil and fastening it in a small quill.

The point used for lettering is generally oil-color, that is color mixed with just enough oil to render it easy-working. Tube colors are not suitable for lettering, as before explained in striping. Quick color may be used when a job is hurried, but it is apt to show laps and brush marks.

We present here, in Fig. 59, some illustrations of various methods of shading.

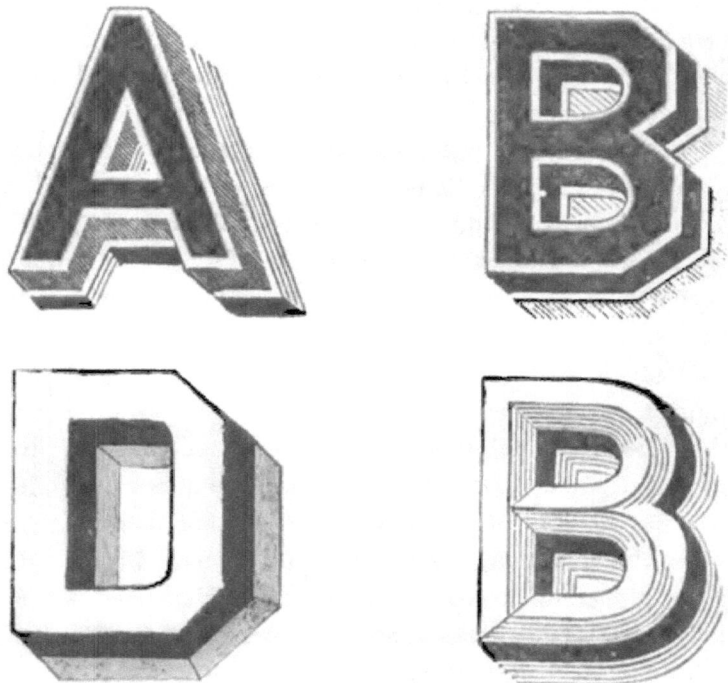

Fig. 59.—*Showing Various Methods of Shading Letters.*

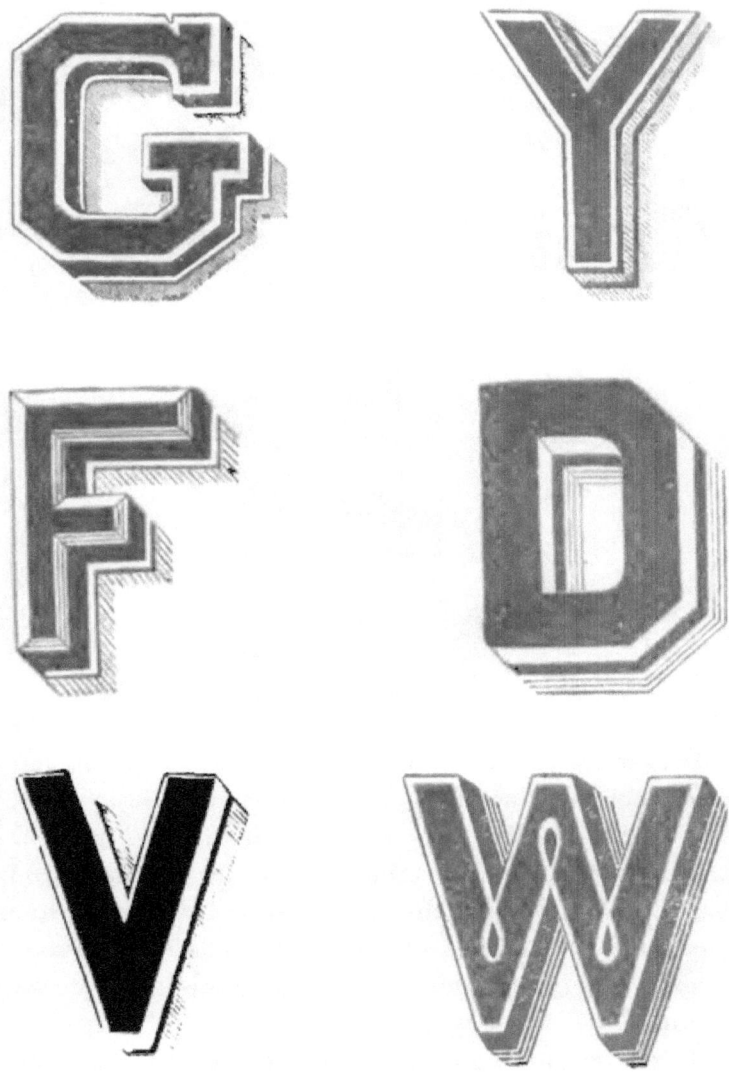

Fig. 59.—*Continued.*

Fig. 59.—Continued.

The operation of gilding is fully explained in our chapter on scrolling, and needs no further allusion here, save that the gold is generally laid on directly from the book. The painter takes the book in the left hand and holding it near the job lifts the paper leaf, then with the point of the book pointing downward, rolls the leaf upon the size, a very easy method when once the knack is acquired.

This brings us to the close of our observations on lettering.

CHAPTER XIII.

WAGON SCROLLING.

Scrolling is an art acquired by but a few. In all the great city of New York those who can design and paint a Roman scroll for wagons, cars, etc., may be counted on the fingers of one hand. Scrolls in relief, or Roman scrolls, require close study, continued practice, and, more than all, an aptitude for such work, natural or inborn, and none may know whether they possess this faculty until they have tried and tried again, following perchance such directions as are here given, or those found in other works of the kind.

The student need not expect to produce at first an elaborate piece of work; he must be content to begin with the rudiments—as in learning music. A blackboard will be found the best for practice, for each line must be drawn with a *free hand*. No means for measuring, other than the eye, should be employed, and he must not be discouraged if he is forced to rub out and try again a hundred times in so simple a task as the drawing of a circle. This drawing of a circle is in fact the key to the whole art of scrolling, for he who can, with a free hand, draw a nearly perfect circle, will be able to form any "sweep" with comparative ease. We illustrate here, in Fig. 60, the first lesson. The line of beauty comes next. This is as shown in Fig. 61, simply a curved line, but unless the curve is made with a graceful turn it does not possess much beauty, and, therefore, it should receive extended practice, until it can be drawn correctly *the first time* in every case.

The next in order is the formation of leafing, giving the

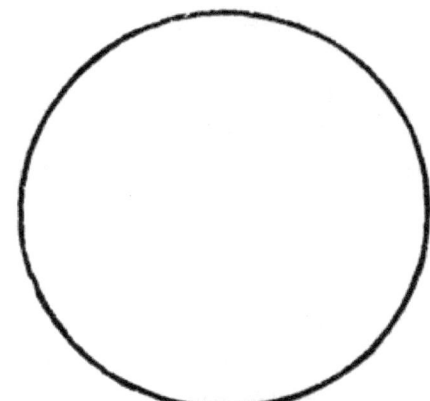

Fig. 60.—The First Lesson in Scrolling.

appearance of a "bend" or "twist" etc. Arabesque or engraved pictures not expressly designed for wagon scrolls should not be copied for this work, for they will in-

Fig. 61.—The Line of Beauty.

variably be found *too fine* or too delicately shaded to supply the want of a wagon painter.

Fig. 62 shows the leafing of a scroll, and the manner of shading to give the appearance of a bend or twist, and in this lesson the student will find employment for a long period, for he should memorize the form, and every line of shade so that without a copy he can make a similar pattern. Originality of design is of importance, and it is

Fig. 62.—*Showing the Leafing of a Scroll and manner of Shading to give the appearance of a Bend or Twist.*

that which gives confidence and a free movement of the pencil, for while the copyist pauses to examine the copy to know what mark to make, he loses the ease and freedom possessed by the original artist, and a certain crudity characterizes his production. The size and form of the panel on which the scroll is to be put at once suggests the form of the scroll, and thus a certain amount of originality will always be demanded from the scroller.

Fig. 63.—*A Shaded Roman Scroll.*

The flat outline of a Roman scroll presents no pleasing form, it is the *shade*, as shown in Fig. 63, which gives it effect. The shading must be done in an off-hand manner, as it is not well to retouch the shading color when once applied. Some work done in color may be an exception to this rule, but in shading gold a retouch of the shade would be plainly seen, and would mar the beauty of the work. Asphaltum is used as the shading on gold and

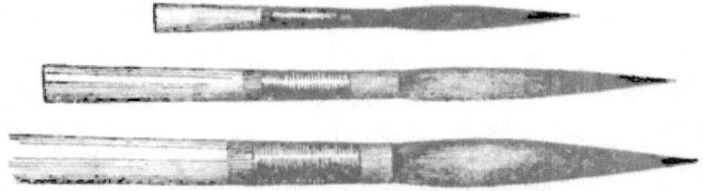

Fig. 64.—Scroll or Lettering Pencils.

it "sets" very quickly. To put on a scroll in gold: First, lightly sketch the design with chalk upon the pounced panel, then, with size as mixed for striping (see Striping) using a sable lettering pencil as shown in Fig. 64, lay on the size, covering the entire surface within the outlines. When the gilding size is "tacky," lay the gold leaf directly from the book—no waxing, greasing, or tip is necessary; lightly rub over with a bunch of soft cotton. Allow sufficient time for the size to become hard, then apply a coat of rubbing varnish over the gold before shading. This gives the painter a chance to wipe off a shade or misplaced line in shading, and it also prevents the asphaltum from striking through or into the gold to give a muddy appearance.

In shading mix a very little burnt sienna with the asphaltum, and thin with brown japan and turpentine, then begin on the tip of a leaf, moving the pencil at right angles with the centre line of the leaf and in a circular manner; continue thus until the broadest part of the leaf is reached, then a few light touches will blend the shade off to the gold. Go all over the design in this manner, then return to that part first done and apply a second coat of shading to those parts requiring to be dark, and sometimes it is well to add a third coat to very dark spots. When the shades are in, the lights (which cannot be shown in the engraving) may be added. The lights consist of fine white or cream colored lines, put on to show where the strongest light strikes the scroll. It will be well for the beginner to study the work of some known professional and learn where the lights are put, as it is impossible for us to show them by engravings, or to explain in words their location.

Heraldic devices, such as spear-heads, quiver and bow, lances, or the heads of animals, are frequently thrown in to improve the appearance of the design, and we often see Scotch-plaid striping used to fill open spaces. But judgment must be exercised, or a gingerbread style will be the result.

We might add just here a few additional suggestions upon designing and laying out scroll patterns, viz.: All curves should be made with an easy, graceful sweep, and harmony must be carefully attended to; for instance, if the design be intended for a centre-piece, circles of the largest diameter should form the centre, and a **gradual** diminution of curves in their various forms be made to extend therefrom until the end or apex is reached on either side. A corner pattern should have the largest circle in the extreme corner. Those who pay particular attention to scrolling, wherever seen, will readily comprehend the ideas we wish to convey.

Again, there should be a similarity between the leaves of a scroll. It would mar the appearance of the work if leaves of various kinds were jumbled together, for, notwithstanding variety breaks monotony, the variety in a scroll design should be made by the various positions of the same kind of leaf. The parts which make up a scroll pattern should be connected, or at least touch each other, and not appear, as they frequently do, as if flying off into space. This is applicable to Roman or relief scrolling more particularly, for it is a common custom in flat scrolling (our next subject) to make many unconnected parts, and in stenciling all parts have to be disconnected in order to form bars or connecting links to hold the parts of the stencil together.

FLAT SCROLLS next demand attention. These are similar to those commonly employed by fresco painters, and do not require the study which Roman or relief scrolls call for. However, there is a certain amount of skill required in order to form pleasing designs. There are three ways of putting on flat scrolls, the first and simplest being in plain gold, with no shades or lights; the second, in various colors, and the third, in colors and gold, but still with no shading. Flat scrolls are *never* shaded, while a scroll in relief always has that peculiarity. The **striping** pencil is often called into requisition in putting on flat scrolls, and he who can execute ornamental striping well, will be equally proficient in this line of scrolling, as it is simply ornamental striping enlarged upon. We present here in Figs. 65, 66, 67 and 68 four designs for flat scrolls, without further remark, referring the reader for additional

Fig. 65.—*Design for a Flat Scroll.*

Fig. 66.—Design for a Flat Scroll.

comments on this subject to our chapters on Ornamental Striping and on Stenciling. Of the latter class of work

Fig. 67.

Fig. 68.

Two Designs for Flat Scrolls.

many parts of flat scrolls may be made, as our remarks under that head will show.

CHAPTER XIV.

STENCILING.

There are many parts of the ornamental work on wagons that can be done with stencils, and much of the ornamental striping and flat scrolling is put on with them. We show in Figs. 69, 70, 71 and 72 the general idea of a stencil. To make them proceed as follows :

Take a sheet of well-calendered writing paper and fold it across the centre, then, with the crease thus formed for a centre of the design, draw on one side of the fold one-half of the pattern with a soft lead pencil, then fold the sheet with the marks inside and laying it on a smooth surface rub over the penciled portion with any smooth, hard substance and the pencil marks will be transferred, making

Fig. 69.— A Stencil Design.

Fig. 70.

Fig. 71.

Fig. 72.

Three Stencil Designs.

the whole pattern. Next, lay the paper on a piece of glass and with a very sharp knife cut out the different parts, being particular to leave bars sufficient to hold the parts together.

The brushes best suited for small stencils of this kind may be purchased at the paint stores, but in case they are not easily procured, take a good-sized camel's hair pencil and cut it square across in the middle. The color should be mixed very stiff in japan, with but little turpentine

Fig. 73.—Brush used in Stenciling.

added, then, dipping the pencil into the paint, rub it out well on a board or piece of paste-board to even the color in the brush. Then, laying the stencil on the desired place, rub the brush over it gently so as not to tear the pattern. The fronts of the spokes are frequently ornamented by the stencil plan, and in Fig. 72 we show a design for that work. Transfer ornaments are extensively used on wagon work, and in some cases are far more economical than hand-work, particularly on spoke faces, and on beds, bars, head-block, etc., of the gears.

SUPPLEMENT.

CARRIAGE PAINTING AND VARNISHING.

[The seven following chapters are from the pen of Mr. C. E. Vader, a practical carriage painter of extended experience, and originally appeared in the columns of the BLACKSMITH AND WHEELWRIGHT. The matter has been carefully revised by Mr. Vader and will form a valuable supplement to Mr. Schriber's experience]:

CHAPTER I.

A GOOD FOUNDATION.

In treating the subject of carriage painting, it is better to begin at the foundation, and consider the first coats that go on a carriage. Of course, this is an old story, and one that has been talked and written about a good deal; but there are many painters who do not think it worth while to bestow much attention on this portion of their work, while I regard it as very important to have the foundation coats well laid on.

In the first place, to make paint stick to wood or iron, it must be elastic, so as to form, as it were, a part of the article to which it is to be applied; and to be elastic it must contain a sufficiency of oil.

Now, I propose to give you my method of painting carriages and wagons, so that paint will not peel or chip off.

When a new set of wheels are to be painted, I first mix the paint with oil, and then add a little japan, the proportion of japan being greater with raw than with boiled oil. Raw oil, I may say right here, is always purer than boiled. I don't always use lead, as, in my opinion, other pigments are just as good, or better. In fact I can never see much difference, if you use oil enough to hold it.

If the wheels or carriage are to be ironed within five days, I put in a few drops of turpentine, but this is not necessary if they are to stand ten days, as in that time they will be in pretty fair condition to sand-paper. It doesn't make so much difference in sand-papering this coat, as we usually take it nearly all off, though this is really not necessary, and your job won't be much better for it. In sand-papering, you should be careful of the corners of spokes, and all other corners. Don't touch a corner if you can help it, and to avoid this, use a very narrow piece of sand-paper around small places.

CHIPPING.

If the paint is going to chip at all, you will notice it first at the corners of the spokes; and when this occurs, there will be nothing to hold the turpentine coats to the bare places on the wood, and unless the difficulty is remedied on the start, the water will get on the wood and cause it to swell. The exposure will start the paint over the exposed parts, and when, on drying, the spokes shrink, the difficulty will be increased. The process of expansion and contraction, if repeated a few times, will cause most of the paint to peel off, leaving spokes and hub nearly bare. If the carriage is much in use, paint so imperfectly applied will not last six months.

THE SECOND COAT.

The second coat should be looked after not less carefully than the first.

I grind my paint in oil, and afterward put in about two tablespoonfuls of good japan (not japan that will curdle) to enough paint to go over a gear and wheels. Then I pour in a little turpentine and mix it very nearly thin enough for working. I commence on this coat with the thumb-nail process, *i. e.*, spread a little paint on the thumb nail, and blow the breath on it for a moment to hasten its drying. If it dries glossy, I add a little more turpentine, so that it will dry with little more than an egg-shell gloss. When there is plenty of time for drying, say six or eight days, I put in all the oil I possibly can, for this coat goes on the bare iron usually, and that, as well as wood, needs all the oil it can get. With this coat I use a 1½ or 2 inch camel's hair brush.

For the first eight or ten hours, this coat will look pretty glossy, the evaporation being very slow, but it will dry out nicely in four or five days if the weather is favorable. It needs at least four days to dry properly. If the job has to be got out in a hurry, I put in more turpentine and less oil. I hardly know which looks the worst, a job that is full of cracks or one that is badly chipped; and one or the other of these evils is sure to be the result if you don't give each coat its proper time to dry.

As there are more coats to go on the body of a carriage than on the gearing, you can easily arrange it so that the gear coats will have more time to dry, and this will enable you to use more oil, which will make your paint tougher and more elastic just where you want it, and, as a consequence, not likely to chip. Such a job will, of course, please a customer; and when a customer is pleased the builder is also pleased, and it is a source of satisfaction to yourself. Nothing is more annoying than to have a job turn up in a year or so with the paint cracking and chipping off, and the customer grumbling about poor work. It doesn't help you much in such cases to **try** to lay the fault to the paint. He has paid you for good paint and good work, and he wants them; and if you wish to keep your customer, there is no way out of the difficulty but to do the job over again. When such things occur, you often wish you had never learned anything about painting, but had turned your attention to farming or almost any other occupation. I have been through all this, and know just what it is, and have learned by experience how such things can be avoided. I worked at the trade with a man who called himself both a house and carriage painter, but he knew very little about carriage painting. I first turned my attention to carriage painting some years ago, when I had nothing else to do. I did not succeed very well on the start, and to try and find ways to overcome the difficulties I met with, I began to study books on painting. The information thus obtained helped me greatly.

PUTTYING.

While my second coat of paint is drying, say two days after being put on, I putty up all open-grained places and imperfections on gear and wheels. Putty for this purpose I make as follows:

Two parts keg lead, one part dry lead, one part umber (the object of which is to color the putty) or two parts dry lead, one part dry whiting, and part keg lead. These I mix with japan and varnish, equal parts, with the addition of a few drops of oil. The oil binds the putty the same as it does paint. Putty should be put on so it will stay, or you can't have good work. If in preparing putty for open-grained spokes you mix it as many do, with japan and turpentine, it soon becomes chalky and flakes off, taking the outside coat of paint with it.

In putting on putty I always plaster it on smooth, so as to avoid the necessity of sand-papering after it is dry.

SAND-PAPERING.

When the second coat has stood as long as possible, say four days at least, I sand-paper it slightly with No. 2 paper, that has been used on other work, and has been worn down nicely. This works better than fine new sand-paper, I think. The object is to scratch the surface of this coat so as to give the one that follows a better chance to take hold firmly.

LAST COAT.

In mixing the third and last coat of paint, I place the pigments in the mill about half an hour before grinding, and pour on turpentine and let them stand. When ready, I add japan, and run the whole through in a stiff mass, screwing the mill pretty tight, so as to grind very fine. By allowing the pigments to stand a little while after pouring on the turpentine, it soaks into and softens them, and the mass can be ground finer.

After grinding, I add a little raw oil, then thin to the proper consistency with turpentine, and go through again with the thumb-nail process described in my last, so as to get the paint into the condition required to have it dry with an egg-shell gloss.

This coat should be laid on very nice and smooth with a hair brush and permitted to dry two or three days. Then I moss it off so as to remove all specks, keeping the corners constantly in mind. Curled hair or moss will take a corner off in a hurry if you rub too hard.

READY FOR GROUND COLOR.

The job is now ready for the ground color, and if it is to be black I use lamp black. It covers the best and is a non-absorbent. This should also be mixed so as to produce the egg-shell gloss, and allow two days for drying.

The next coat is the color proper. I use the ground ivory black, best quality. Take out the required amount of black in a clean cup and mix it carefully with a stick. The sticks I prepare on purpose for mixing. I think I can mix paint better with one of these prepared sticks than with a putty knife, as they fit up to the side of the cup and mash the colors better.

Turpentine should be added little by little (not poured all in at once) till you have obtained the right consistency. Then add raw oil, and test the paint on your thumb nail in order to be sure you are going to have the egg-shell gloss when dry.

DRYING DEAD.

Many painters have an idea that these coats of black should contain no oil, so that they may dry dead. I was taught to put on color in this way, and supposed it must be put on so, but reading up on the subject gave me some new ideas. I commenced experimenting and watching not only my own work but the work of others, and found a great many cases of color chipping off from the last coat of lead. I soon discovered the reason of this and will explain it. Take some color mixed with turpentine and japan, and lay it on a piece of tin or anything that will spring. Let it dry, and then bend the tin or other article a little, and the paint will crack in every direction, and in most cases will fly nearly all off. Now add some oil, and paint your piece of tin and you can scarcely make it crack by bending. The oil toughens the paint and imparts elasticity to it. This illustration makes it plain why paint not properly mixed will peel off a carriage. Very many parts of a carriage will spring and vibrate sufficiently to destroy paint that is hard and unyielding.

With this last coat dry, the job is ready for the **varnish coats**.

THE VARNISH COATS.

I take rubbing varnish and add drop black to make the varnish black. This keeps the varnish from "greening" the paint when the job is done. I take the black from the can as it is ground, and do not put any turpentine in to thin it. The best way is to grind dry black in varnish. If drop black is ground in good Japan, it will mix with varnish and stand better without cracking than if ground in poor Japan. Japan or turpentine never works with varnish very well any way. I always use a badger hair brush in varnishing, but some prefer bristle and fitch to wipe up with. I flow on a medium heavy coat, dress it, and lay it on as smoothly as if it were the last or finishing coat. This coat should stand at least two days, and three or four will be much better, if possible, it will rub so much nicer. I rub this a little with pulverized pumice stone and water, to remove gloss and specks. These specks should be few and scattering, and they will be if the job is clean and the room kept clean. In my estimation, there is more dirt on a job when the varnishing is done than gets on afterward.

If the job is not a very particular one, I simply rub it with curled hair. After being rubbed with pumice stone it should be washed very clean, and the next coat of clear rubbing varnish laid on. This should also be put on very nicely and smoothly, and should stand three or four days, if possible, before rubbing it with pumice stone and water. (I should have said that if the job has to be striped it should be put on over color varnish.)

THE FINISHING COAT.

Now we are ready for the finishing coat. I use a good, first-class grade of varnish all through, and always of one company's make. Then I know how long it takes to dry out of the way of dust, and how long before it can be run out.

The job should have a good cleaning and dusting before attempting to varnish. This should be laid on quite heavy, and dressed so there will be no runs or sags when dry, and then our job will be completed.

A great many might say the method I have attempted to describe makes a job too long, and differ with me in the time I allow for drying. Of course we cannot give so much time for every job, but I am trying to give my plan of laying out a job, instead of letting one coat stand three weeks and then putting on the five or six coats in a week.

PAINTING BODIES.

When the body is received from the body shop it should

be well dusted off and a coat of lead or other pigment mixed with raw oil and japan (one part japan and three parts raw oil) applied to it. Leave the inside two or three days. After the body is hung up (as it should be before it is rough-stuffed) it should be sand-papered down smooth, and a second coat of lead laid on, mixed with the pigment ground in oil, and two tablespoonfuls of japan added, and thinned with turpentine. Give this two days to dry, and then apply a coat with less oil in it. In twenty-four hours it will be ready for the rough-stuff. Nearly every painter has a recipe of his own for this paint, but mine is: To three parts filler add one part keg lead, two parts of japan, two parts rubbing varnish, the whole run through the mill in a stiff mass, and afterwards thinned with turpentine. This should be laid on thin, and about six coats altogether, one each day, with two days to dry and rub down.

RUBBING.

The fine finish of a body depends a great deal on the rubbing, and it should be rubbed carefully, and not left to an inexperienced hand. After it is rubbed it should stand twenty-four hours to dry out, or over night will do if it is drying weather or the room is warm. I mix lamp black for ground work with raw oil one part, japan two parts, run through the mill and thinned with turpentine, and try it on the thumb nail to see that it dries with a gloss. Paint has to be oily when put over rough-stuff to dry with an eggshell gloss, as the rough-stuff soaks up the oil; and you might as well put more oil in this coat and give it more time to dry as to give it a coat of oil lead before you put on the lamp black, I think. At least, I like to see it dry with a little gloss, as it holds out the varnish coats better. I let this dry two days, and apply a coat of drop black mixed so as to dry with a subdued gloss. Give this twelve or eighteen hours to dry, and put on a coat of color varnish. (I prefer black varnish to color varnish.) Give this two days, then rub lightly with pumice stone; stripe and ornament, and apply a coat of clear rubbing. Give this three days to dry.

This varnish does not need so much rubbing as some suppose. If it is put on level it will not need much rubbing to make a nice finish. Unless this is a very nice job I only put on two coats of rubbing, or three in all. After this is rubbed I apply the finishing coat immediately, and the job is done.

CHAPTER II.

DUSTING AND CLEANING WORK.

Before Applying Paint or Varnish.—There is perhaps nothing more annoying to the carriage painter than to turn out a vehicle, having its beautiful surface covered with specks or dirt. He takes great care with all his work up to the varnish coats. Then comes the time when dust will show itself. After the job is done, and set up, the painter will see at a glance how much dirt or dust there is imbedded in the varnish, and will say to himself (sometimes aloud to others):

"I don't see where that dirt came from? I had a clean cup, and my brush was clean, and my clothes I dusted off as well as the job. There must have been some one in the room after I left, but I locked the door and had the key in my pocket. Perhaps there was dirt in the varnish." And he will fidget and wonder where the dirt came from, and will perhaps think of all these things. But he doesn't think enough ; he doesn't think deep enough. He lets it pass this time as the mischief is done, and he has not time to let it stand ten days to rub down and apply another coat. Probably next time it will come out better.

Now you painters who have trouble with dirt let us talk this matter over, and see if we can't find out where the trouble lays. Go back to the first coat of black that is to go on a body. The job has stood twenty-four hours after being rubbed out of rough stuff. The surface is all grit, you can tell that by rubbing your hand over it. You take a common duster and go over it, and perhaps think it is clean. Pass your hand over it again, and, if you watch close, you will feel a fine grit. Now if you should put a coat of paint over this as it is, while you were applying the paint you would see hundreds of little fine specks. The more you brushed and worked the paint on the panels, the more these specks would show. These minute particles are rolled over and over in the paint, and every time they are rolled over they grow larger, and what could hardly be seen with the naked eye at first, will seem quite large when your paint is applied. Now, before applying your paint, you should take a very fine piece of sand-paper and rub the surface slightly, and dust off with a common duster. Then take a piece of curled hair (not moss), and dampen it in varnish (oil will do); squeeze it out so that no varnish will rub off, and rub this over your work slightly. Next take a bristle duster, put a little varnish in the palm of your hand, and rub the ends of the bristles in the varnish, so it will adhere. Rub this duster over the work and the dirt or grit will adhere to it, and be all taken up by it. Now your work is in a condition to apply the paint. If the paint is the least bit specky, or has any pieces of skin on top, it should be strained through a piece of book-muslin into a clean cup and applied with a clean brush. One more important thing is to get the job where the dust will not be settling on it when it is drying.

The next coat should be gone through with almost in

the same way. At least, be sure there is no dirt on the job when you apply the paint.

When the first coat of varnish is rubbed with pumice stone it is very difficult to get it all out of corners of moldings and such places. It should be washed out, and water run into these places freely, and with a sash-tool clean out all the stone you can, and wipe dry. When the job has stood ten minutes, look around the corners and you will discover enough stone to spoil four or five jobs. I have seen painters take the "shammy" and run one corner of it into these places, and of course it would dampen the stone, and give the work the appearance of being clean, when perhaps hardly a particle of stone had been removed. They would then dust off with a common duster, without seeming to think about or look after the places any more, and immediately apply the varnish. Of course, the first time the brush went in one of these corners it would take out some of the powdered stone, and in brushing the varnish they would scatter these fine particles in all directions, and when rolled in varnish several times over, they will look five times as large as they really are. The job would have very much the appearance of having been sprinkled with fine pepper.

PUTTING UP JOINTS.

When you have a job that has open joints, such as where the seat is screwed to the body, these joints should be puttied up so they will be smooth. On iron seats, around handles, there are many open places. If these are puttied up they will clean very easy. When the job has stood a few moments after rubbing, take a common duster and dust all over—not rubbing too hard ; now go over again in the same way. If you have a magnifying glass, look over the work and see if you discover any dirt. In nine cases out of ten it will look as if it had not been dusted. Now, in most cases, right here is the dirt that makes your job look bad when finished. Nearly always a job is as dirty when you get done varnishing as it is when dry.

Of course, there are cases where a job is got out clean, and dust gets on it while drying, from the wind shaking the shop, or something of this kind. Most country shops are affected by wind, and, unless the room is very tight, dust will sift out. One thing is certain, if the job is not clean, it is impossible to get a clean finish. After your job has been dusted with a common duster, take another duster, and put a little varnish in your hand, rub the points of the duster with it, and go over the work with this, being particular about the corners and moldings. Then have a 2½-inch flat bristle brush, that has never been in paint, and rub varnish on the points of this, and you can clean your job perfectly. Keep this brush close by you, and rub it over a panel just before the varnish. Of course it requires three times as long to dust and get a job clean as it does to lay on the varnish.

CLEANING GEARS.

In cleaning gears considerable pains should be taken, although dust will not show as much as on bodies or large surfaces. A flat bristle brush should be used after the duster, the same as on bodies ; and be particular to go around clips and ends of the springs. Run the bristles into every little place. One important thing, in my estimation, is to start from a certain place, and go from one clip to another. Commence at one end of a spring and go to the other, and so on around, and then you will know when you get through, and that every spot has been touched. System is as important in carriage painting as in any other line of business.

CHAPTER III.

PAINTING LUMBER WAGONS.

The woodwork should be primed before it is ironed. When this has been done give the wagon a slight sanding with No. 2 sand-paper. Clean the grease and coal cinders off the iron parts. Mix lead and Indian red, employing two parts of lead and one part of Indian red. Thin up with turpentine and put in about two tablespoonfuls of Japan and as much oil in a quantity sufficient for a wagon. Apply this quite heavy, touching every part, using a good bristle brush. It is seldom that lumber wagons receive two coats before the color is applied. It makes more durable work, however, to put on two coats of the paint just described. Next take American vermilion, deep shade, and mix it with Japan and oil, using equal parts, to a stiff mush. Thin this with turpentine. Take one part whiting in bulk to two parts of vermilion. Mix the whiting to a stiff mush with oil and run through the mill. Thin up and mix with the vermilion. This is an important matter and should not be left out, as the whiting makes vermilion work like other paint. Vermilion being very heavy, it settles rapidly and settles after being put on, as well as before, and thereby makes the work look spotted. It will be a hard task for one not used to putting on this paint to make one coat cover satisfactorily. It requires to be worked very fast and even. The paint must be kept even in thickness.

STRIPING.

The day succeeding the operations just described the work will be ready to stripe. The colors for this should be black and white, or instead of the latter, light yellow. White makes the red show off to the best advantage. Take lamp black and mix with japan and oil in equal parts. Thin up with turpentine. Silver or flake white in tubes is best for the white, using turpentine as a dipper. This stripe will dry over night.

A GOOD COLOR.

Straw or buff is a popular color for wagons. It is easily worked and is a good paint to wear. It may be made of lead and ochre and shaded to suit. Three coats make a satisfactory job. Wagon boxes should be primed with lead and a little lamp black before being ironed; then given a good sand-papering with No. 2 sand-paper. Then apply another coat of lead color. The best color for boxes is brown. Green has been used to a considerable extent, but it does not make a wagon as attractive as a rich brown.

Venetian red and lamp black make a good brown. Indian red and lamp black constitute a little richer shade. If the very best shade is wanted use drop black and Indian red. Yellow of different shades and English vermilion make the most showy stripes for such boxes. Blue and green are also attractive.

READY TO VARNISH.

At this stage the whole wagon is ready for the varnish which should be a good article of coach varnish. Black, sticky stuff should not be employed. As heavy a coat as possible should be put on, care being taken to wipe out thoroughly around the bolt heads and around the irons, Lay the boards flat down and lay on the varnish heavy and lay off cross-wise of boards, then set them off on horses flat down. Left in this position the varnish will not run. By so doing a heavier coat can be applied than otherwise. The inside of the boxes should be painted with Venetian red and oil, one or two coats.

CHAPTER IV.

TOUCHING UP REPAIR WORK.

Blacksmiths and woodworkers have occasion quite often to touch up their repair work with paint, when there is not time for the job to be finished in the paint shop. Some men have paint dishes in the shop to use themselves as may be necessary, while in other shops the painters attend to these things. Very often this takes a painter away from something he can't leave very well, while some of the other hands could have done it while he was coming down stairs. But blacksmiths and woodworkers generally daub up and do more damage than good in their attempts at painting. We have a spoke or two that must be used immediately; if it is black we generally put on black varnish, but paint, dark lead or something heavy would be much better. Black varnish will come off gradually and won't keep the grain from raising; of course, it has a little shine, but you can't get one coat on very well without making it look streaked. So, take it on the whole, it doesn't look very well and it is in no shape to paint up again.

But whatever is put on should be applied properly; if you have a large brush and the paint or varnish is old and sticky and you daub all over, it looks bad, besides making lots of work for the painter when the job comes to be painted. You can't get this stuff off, even a spot of it when it gets dry without the use of a sharp knife, and you can hardly ever succeed in preventing a spot that will show always. The paint should be mixed with oil, japan and turpentine in equal parts, or keg lead and lamp black mixed with japan and turpentine. It should be mixed up once a week, so as to be fresh, and dry quickly and well. Have an inch and a half bristle brush, not an old stick of a thing, but a good brush, and keep it soft in the paint or water. A spoke is about the worst thing to get around without touching the hub or other spokes, but take a brush half full of paint and put down as near the hub as possible, and then tip up the brush a little and work crosswise of the spoke and you will touch all bare wood without getting on the old paint. If you should, why wipe it off with a rag or finger. Go around the butt of the spoke in this way, then at the felloe to the same, cutting close, and then fill in between hub and felloe and smooth up nicely. This will, perhaps, take a moment longer on a spoke, but it will be enough better to pay.

When a smith heats an iron that has been painted, and doesn't heat the whole of it, the paint will fry up black a little ways and cinders will stick. These should be filed or sand-papered off and dusted or rubbed off with the hand before the paint is applied. If you will only take a little pains and work slow around these places at first you will soon get so you can do it about as quick as if you were merely daubing. One should take as much pains in patching up a job as he would in making a new article, but there are not many who do. When taking off clips on irons on a painted job the paint is liable to break up away from the clip. Now if you will take a knife with a sharp point and cut around the clip it will come and go right back, and will not need to be touched up. When hammering or pounding on a painted iron or surface, take a piece of harness leather and hold it under the hammer; remember that an ounce of prevention is worth a pound of cure.

CHAPTER V.

HOW TO PAINT A CHEAP JOB.

Sometimes we want to paint a job cheap, or not lay out much work on it. Sometimes blacksmiths or wagon-makers want to do a job themselves, and are at a loss to know just how to go to work at it. I will give my way of doing such work.

PAINTING AN EXPRESS WAGON.

Let us suppose that we are going to paint an express wagon or a spring wagon of any kind. All wood work should be primed with keg lead or any pigment ground in oil. Venetian red, Indian red, umber, or any of these dry paints, will do. After taking out a little in a cup (enough to make a pint when mixed) put in about two tablespoonfuls of japan and stir with a stick rounded at the end or made oval to fit the side of the cup. Stir this until all the lumps disappear; then add about as much turpentine as japan, thin with oil and try on wood. Raw oil will be best, as it dries quickest, and holds better. It should be thinned until it will streak on the wood with the brush. It should not cover thoroughly. Above all, do not use old paint that has stood around in dishes and become fatty. Such paint should be used only on the inside of boxes or bottoms. After the wagon is ironed, sand-paper with No. 2 sand-paper. That which has been used by the woodworker is best. It need not be rubbed too much; just enough to smooth nicely. The body will need more sand-papering if it is not rough stuffed. Sand-paper down so the first coat will be nearly off, as this fills the grain up.

THE GEAR COAT.

The next coat, for gear, I would mix in this wise: Take out lead enough for a pint of paint, or the dish nearly a third full. Put in two tablespoonfuls of best japan and stir well. Then add the same quantity of raw oil and stir again. Thin with turpentine. It should not have much, as in sanding many places are left bare, and it should be elastic so it will stick well. This should be applied with an inch and a half camel's hair brush. It can be done with a bristle brush, but a camel's hair costs no more, and the paint can be spread more evenly, and it will go farther and can be thinned more. It should be made as thin as possible and cover good.

PAINT FOR BODY.

The paint for the body will need no oil, as there is enough in keg lead to bind it. The body will not receive so many jars as the gearing. About the same amount of japan should be put in and thinned with turpentine. All screw and nail holes should be puttied a day or two before you are to paint, or it can be done the next day after the priming is put on. The putty make with dry lead, whiting and Venetian red or umber, equal parts, mixed with japan and varnish and a little turpentine. A better finish can be obtained by plastering the body all over with this putty, made thin. It can be put on with an old plane iron if you have no plaster knife. This paint should be applied with a camel's hair brush if possible.

It can be put on with the one you paint gears with, but a two-inch brush would be much better and enable you to work faster. If the body is plastered, this coat should be put over the putty coat after being sand-papered. Now it is all ready for the ground, when it is well dried. If some colors are used on the gear, like Indian red, or light brown made with Indian red and lampblack, Portland umber and the like, there will be no particular necessity for having a ground, as these are very strong and will cover solid over almost any priming coats. But it is a good plan to govern the priming according to the color the gear is to be painted. Portland umber, or stone color, can be made of ochre and umber, toned to suit the taste, or ochre, Venetian red and black. These should be ground in japan and oil, equal parts. They can be obtained already ground in oil; then japan should be added, thin with turpentine, and apply with the brush used in first coats, provided you have but one camel's hair brush; wash in turpentine and rub well into the color.

PAINTING THE BODY.

The body will look best painted a dark brown, made of Indian red and drop black. A man accustomed to laying paint would make one coat over, but an inexperienced hand would do best to put on two coats, one in the morning and one at night; or, if there is plenty of time, give a day to each coat. This will only need a little oil to bind it. The body will need two coats of varnish, the first put on after the color is dry. It can be striped and ornamented the next day.

The gear will do with one coat of varnish, so it should be striped over the color, and will now be ready for the finishing coat of varnish, which should be laid on quite heavy. It should be varnished with a pretty good varnish. Coach varnish will hardly do, as it does not wear long enough and cracks quickly. Good, reliable varnish can be obtained at almost any hardware store. It will cost a little more than common varnish, but is cheaper in the end.

CHAPTER VI.

HOW TO REVARNISH A CARRIAGE.

After the carriage has been well washed from dirt, unhang the body and give it another thorough washing. Let the body dry for twenty-four hours. Give the gear a thorough washing, and rub it down with ground pumice stone. By this means all grease and specks, which would otherwise remain, will be removed. This treatment of the gear is a very particular job. The rubbing should be carefully watched. After a wheel or part of the gear has been rubbed, it should be washed, in order that the pumice stone may not adhere to it. The pumice stone should never be allowed to dry upon the work. Give all the parts a good washing, and clean well in the corners with a sash tool. Wipe dry with a chamois skin. After all the parts have been thus gone over, set aside twenty-four hours to dry. I think it a good plan at the outset, if there is no mud on the carriage, to dust off and apply paint to the bare places before washing. This will prevent the moisture penetrating the wood to a great extent during the washing.

All bare places should be painted with lead, or some other heavy paint. They require two or three coats, in order to bring them up to a good surface. At least one coat will be necessary on small bare places. Otherwise the color will not stick.

After the lead is dry the touching begins. This is no easy job, and accordingly it should not be left to an inexperienced person. If the job is not black, the first thing necessary to be done is to match the color. This is sometimes quite a trying task. In some instances it is found impossible to match the color exactly. This is frequently the case where such colors as lake, red, or blue have been used, and have faded while in use. In such cases there is no better way to do than to come as near as possible to the color and let it go at that. A job originally painted black will turn green after a year or more exposure, or at least will manifest a greenish hue. In such cases the touches should be as small as possible, so that they will not be too prominent when the job is finished.

In touching up the body, if there are moldings or beads, they should be gone around with a small brush of color to set the dirt in places where it is hard to get out. A body in most places requires two coats of varnish, for the reason that it is almost impossible to varnish a body over once without the dirt coming out in the varnish. Whatever care may be taken in the preliminary cleaning there will always be this trouble to meet. In two-coat work the first coat may be rubbed down with stone, and by this means the dirt rubbed away. Upon this foundation there will be no difficulty in finishing, if the final coat is put on nicely.

There is something about touching up and re-varnishing a carriage from which every painter shrinks. He dislikes to engage in such work, for it is practically impossible to make it look as good as new. Frequently the owner is not satisfied, believing it might have been done better. Unless a carriage is in very good condition and not much faded it should be repainted, even if but one coat of color varnish is applied, and one coat of varnish to finish.

CHAPTER VII.

[The matter forming this chapter was written by Mr. Petersen, and originally appeared in the French journal *Le Peintre en Voiture*.]

FORMS AND COLORS IN THE PAINTING OF VEHICLES.

A correct appreciation of the relations which exist between form and color is a qualification much needed by a painter of vehicles.

He should clearly understand that color must invariably be subordinate to form. There are some forms which will fail to display all the beauty inherent in them unless they have the accompaniment of brilliant coloring. The angular or regular forms are examples of this law.

Then there are other forms which appear best in faint or subdued colors.

The only regular form which is found in the human body is the circle of the eye, and that is the only part to which nature ever imparts a brilliant color.

The savage with his body painted red, yellow or blue is hideous, but the wing of the butterfly, the plumage of the humming bird are beautiful.

Even among the flowers, those possessing regular forms are always the most brilliant colored, and as the forms depart from regularity so the colors become delicate or subdued.

BRIGHT COLORS FOR BUGGIES AND DOG-CARTS.

The buggy and dog-cart appear best when painted in bright colors, but cabriolets and mail coaches require dark or subdued colors. The two first named vehicles are composed of straight lines and regular forms but the two last, though differing from one another in many respects, are alike in being made in semicircles and curves of various forms.

We have often seen dog-carts and buggies which displeased the eye, simply because their bodies were painted in colors too subdued, while others were agreeable to the sight, because their bright coloring was in harmony with their regular forms.

It would therefore be well for painters of vehicles to remember that straight lines demand brilliant coloring, while curves, etc., are most effective in subdued or delicate colors

ONE COLOR FOR WOOD AND ANOTHER FOR IRON.

When more colors than one are employed in painting a vehicle, it is usual to make the body of one color and the wheels of another, and this is not a bad method. The distinction made between the parts mentioned seems a natural one, and the difference in their colors generally gives the vehicle a light and handsome appearance.

But this is not the only way in which the painting of a vehicle may be varied. At one time there could often be seen carriages in which the wooden parts were all of the same color, as for instance yellow, while the iron portions were all of another color—perhaps black.

Thus painted these carriages look well, for although the

difference between the wood and the iron is not so apparent as that between the body and wheels of a vehicle, still it is a point which should be always remembered by the painter.

Some American carriages are so painted as to make the metallic axles of the same color as the wooden spokes of the wheels.

It is to be presumed that in working in this fashion the painter's object is to make two different materials appear to be one and the same. But such dissimulation is in bad taste. Good taste is always true and straightforward, hiding nothing and counterfeiting nothing, making every material appear at its best, but never attempting to bring one substance into an apparent resemblance to something very different.

It has been argued that painting the wooden and iron parts of the same color gives a lighter appearance to the vehicle. But unfortunately it does this and more; it makes the vehicle seem too light. Every one knows that the strain on an axle is very much greater than that which a spoke has to sustain, and yet the former is not much larger than the latter. Consequently the spoke appears too large or the axle too small. But when the axle is painted of a different shade from the spoke, the fact that the one is wood and the other iron, and therefore equal to its task, is at once apparent.

Now it is a fact that when some of these American carriages are seen in the streets they seem to an inexperienced observer to be too weak for actual use. A carriage maker does not make this mistake, because he instinctively recognizes the difference in the materials employed.

For these reasons, we think that under all circumstances the metallic parts of a vehicle should be painted of a different color from that employed on the wood.

CRITICISM ON THE ABOVE BY A CORRESPONDENT OF "LE PEINTRE EN VOITURE"—ALL PARTS OF A CARRIAGE SHOULD BE OF SAME COLOR.

In my opinion no painter should seek to indicate by colors the difference in the materials of a vehicle. I believe that an appearance of strength and solidity can be best attained by using the same color for all parts, and thereby avoiding a too prominent exhibition of joints, bolts, etc.

I think that another result of making the body one color and the carriage part another is the loss of harmony, and without harmony there can be but little beauty. I do not assert that there are no such things as agreeable contrasts, but there are also contrasts which do not please all eyes; and when the painter deviates from harmony, even in a small degree, he is liable to produce effects more odd than beautiful.

I contend that when the carriage part is painted of a brighter color than the body the vehicle may appear gay, but certainly not elegant. Take, for instance, a type of carriage to be seen every day. Its proportions are good: the body is painted brown and the panels are encircled by a fine line of gold. The carriage part is light brown, set off by a large black band which has two white lines in its centre; the naves, spokes and moldings of the wood are decorated in gold. What ridiculous taste is here displayed! Now behold another vehicle; the panels and carriage part are of a rich shade of green, set off by large black bands bordered by a narrow straw-colored line, thus forming a partial contrast. The *ensemble* is green and black, lightened by a line of yellow as a contrast. Thus painted the general effect is decidedly pleasing, but if the yellow line is removed and one of bright green substituted, the result is harmony, and consequently elegance. If, on the contrary, a red line is employed instead of the green, the effect is ridiculous.

Another happy contrast can be produced by using black for the ground color, and setting it off with blue *glacé*, or the body might be in brown *glacé* and the carriage part in brilliant carmine set off by a black band. There is a strong contrast between the brown and the carmine, and yet the two colors harmonize, because they both approach the red.

Let us now consider a combination which shall be thoroughly harmonious, for instance a body in brown *glacé*, with the moldings set off by a narrow line of carmine, the carriage part to be painted like the body, and with a black band, on each side of which (but not very close) is a narrow line of carmine.

Yet to return to your remarks in the last number, in spite of the incontestably elegant appearance of this carriage, the method of painting adopted would tend to make it appear as if all the parts were composed of the same material.

But it seems to me that to paint the wooden parts in one color and the iron in another would be a very poor method of obtaining an appearance of strength. A spectator not acquainted with the construction of carriages, so far from being impressed by the apparent solidity of such a vehicle, would be more likely to conceive just the opposite opinion. I should certainly consider my life safer in a carriage that looked firm and compact than one in which every joint was made prominent by its color. I do not care to have my carriage appear as if it could be taken apart off-hand and carried around like a fishing rod.

In conclusion let me say that an observer so ignorant as to suppose that a vehicle lacks strength, because it appears light, should be advised to seek instruction on the subject, and if he refuses to do so we can only say to him "*Au revoir*," for science should make **no** compromise with an ignoramus. F. J. G.

REJOINDER BY MR. PETERSEN.

THE HARMONY OF ANALOGY.

My remarks on the subject of the painting of the wooden and iron parts of vehicles have drawn from F. J. G. a criticism which I will now proceed to answer.

The first comment I have to make is that his taste evidently differs from mine. He prefers a combination of colors which I would term the harmony of analogy, and which consists in a decided color for the bottom, relieved by slight but not marked variations from this tint and sometimes by the occasional use of a neutral color, black or white. This method of painting is now much in vogue and produces an elegant effect when the painter who adopts it possesses the necessary taste and skill, and it is especially well suited for carriages in which curves and irregular forms predominate, because the grace of such hues and curves render a richer and more marked style of painting useless if not superfluous. But if the painter who follows this method lacks discrimination in the choice of his colors or ability in applying them, the result is a disagreeable faintness and indistinctness. Moreover, no skill or taste in the application can make this style of painting successful on carriages characterized by straight or angular forms; for in such cases bright, decided colors are indispensable.

THE HARMONY OF CONTRASTS.

F. J. G. appears to suppose that the harmony of analogy is the only one which exists in colors. He is mistaken. It is the first, simplest and most natural manner of varying painting, but it is not the only one. The harmony of contrasts is employed in accordance with the laws of colors is a higher, richer and more artistic method of ornamentation. Of course the successful employment of the harmony of contrasts demands a careful, skillful consideration of tones and proportions, and when these points are neglected the results are not satisfactory. Still we fail to see why colors that are too brilliant or decided are worse than a combination of faint, insignificant tints.

CHAPTER VIII.

TRANSFER ORNAMENTS.

Transfers or "Decalcomanie," as it is sometimes called, are so well known that they require but a passing word. Some beautiful designs have of late come to our notice, and it is indeed surprising how the art has grown within the past few years. We can now procure a beautiful scroll and landscape for the sides of an omnibus or wagon, the whole figure (consisting of an oval centre and six parts of scroll, which can be put either in a straight line, or combined to fit any curve, 14 inches wide and 92 inches in length), costing only $7.50. Scrolls 18 or 20 inches, in gold and colors, are now no rarity, and when well applied to a job give elegance for a trifling expense. We speak more particularly of the large transfers, and advise their use where such designs cannot be readily drawn, because they are not so likely to be known as transfers, owing to their size and beautiful workmanship. They are indeed very different from the carriage ornaments such as every little schoolboy had at one time stuck on everything, both in school and at home.

A transfer ornament may be so changed in appearance that it would never be known as such, by a few touches of the pencil, the slight addition occupying but little time.

HOME-MADE TRANSFERS.

It frequently occurs that a carriage owner desires a very

elaborate coat-of-arms on his carriage panel, and yet cannot spare the carriage long enough for the artist to do the work. Now to get over this trouble:

Procure a sheet of gummed paper (similar to a postage stamp), and upon the gummed surface paint the design in the same manner and with the same colors as would be used on the carriage panel. Let it dry ; then slightly wetting or dampening another piece of the gummed paper, lay the painted design face down upon it and press it between the leaves of a book until dry. Next, dampen the back of the paper on which the design was painted, and when soft enough remove it, in the same manner as when using an ordinary transfer. This leaves the painted design face downward upon the gummed paper similar to any other transfer.

When the home-made transfers are thus completed, send for the carriage and transfer the design to the panels by varnishing the back with transfer varnish, or a little rubbing varnish. Dampen and remove the paper as usual, and you will find the design as nicely depicted on the panel as if it were a purchased decalcomanie, and the time taken to do such work would be nothing, compared to the painting done on the carriage itself.

This plan of operations might be utilized by the painter for other work. He might take home some little job of this kind, and make money in spare moments.

MONOGRAMS

We present in the following pages some specimens of monograms of various styles and sizes.

English.

Florentine.

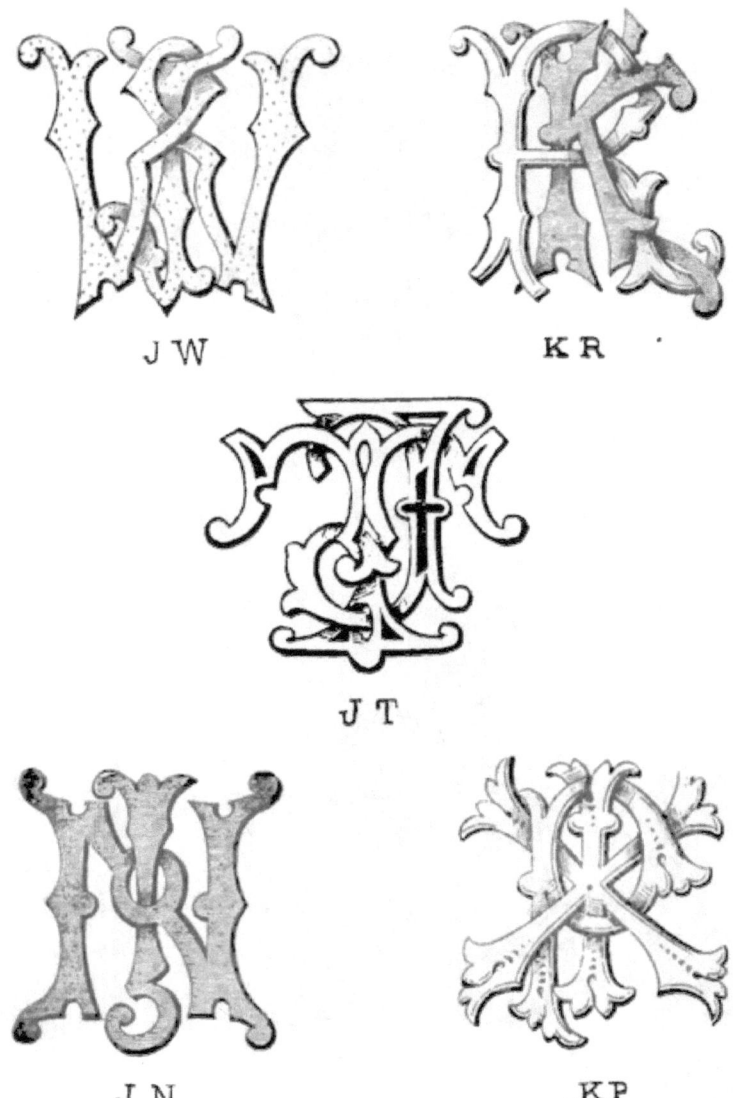

J.S.   K M.   K.G.   J P   K O

Modern.

Louis XV.

INDEX.

	PAGE.
Benches and Boxes for Colors	17
Blacking off Ribs	63
Brushes, Badger Hair	15
Brushes, "Bridling"	13, 14
Brushes, Cleaning up	16
Brushes, Flat Bristle	16
Brushes for Painting	13 to 16
Brushes, Oval	15, 16
Brushes used in a Cheap Job	149, 150
Brushes used in Varnishing	42
Brush, Camel's Hair	14, 15
Carmine, Cheap Substitutes for	49
Chipping	128
Chipping from Last Coat	132, 133
Color, Bismarck Brown	23
Color, Bottle Green	21
Color, Brick	23
Color, Bronze Green	23
Color, Brown	22
Color, Canary	21
Color, Carnation Red	23
Color, Chamoline	23
Color, Chestnut	22
Color, Chocolate	23
Color, Citron	22
Color, Claret	22
Color, Clay Drab	23
Color, Coffee	22
Color, Cream	22
Color, Dark Milori Green	23
Color, Dark Rich Brown	24
Color, Deep Buff	21
Color, Dove	22
Color, Drab	22
Color, Fawn	22
Color, Flesh	22
Color, French Gray	21

	PAGE.
Color, French Red	23
Color, Gold	21
Color, Grass Green	23
Colors, Grinding	25, 26
Color, Japan Brown	24
Color, Jonquil Yellow	23
Color, Le Cuir or Leather	24
Color, Lemon	22
Color, Light Buff	21
Color, Light Gray	22
Color, Lilac	22
Color, London Smoke	22
Color, Maroon	22
Color, Medium Gray	21
Colors, Mixing	19 to 26
Color, Oak	21
Color, Olive	21
Color, Olive Brown	23
Color, Peach Blossom	23
Color, Pea Green	22
Color, Pearl	21
Color, Plum	23
Color, Portland Stone	23
Color, Primrose Yellow	24
Color, Purple	22
Color, Ready mixed	17, 18
Color, Rose	21
Color, Salmon	21
Color, Snuff	21
Color, Stone	22
Color, Straw	22
Color, Tan	22
Color, Tea Green	24
Color, Violet	22
Color, Willow Green	22
Color, Willow Leaf Green	24
Color, Wine	22
Color, Yellow Lake	23
Color and Form in Vehicles	155 to 159
Colors (Bright) for Straight Line Vehicles	**156**
Colors Elegantly Combined in a Vehicle, An Illustration of	**159**
Colors Employed on Wagons	**68, 69**
Colors for Buggies and Dog Carts	**156**
Colors for Cabriolets and Mail Coaches	**156**

INDEX.

	PAGE.
Colors for Lumber Wagon Boxes	143
Colors for Striping	55
Color for Wood Should Not be the Same as for Iron	156
Colors (Subdued) for Vehicles made in Curved Lines	156
Color Subordinate to Form	155
Colors Suitable for First Coat, on a Business Wagon Body	34, 35, 36
Colors, to Match, in Re-varnishing	153
Colors used for Business Wagon Gears	36
Colors used for the Second Coat on a Business Wagon Body	36
Colors used for Striping Lumber Wagons	143
Colors used in Wagon Painting	17, 18
Colors used on Delivery Wagons	68, 69
Colors used on Ribbed Body Business Wagons	68
Drying, Dead	132, 133
Dusting and Cleaning Work	137, 138, 139, 140, 141
Dutch Metal	67
Edging Gold Letters	107
Ellipse, How to Make	101 to 103
Ellipse, Use of, in Making Round Letters	97
Figures, Balancing Properly	103
Finish for End of Panel Stripe	62, 63
Foundation in Carriage Painting	127, 128
Furniture of Paint Rooms	12, 13
Furniture of Varnish Rooms	12, 13
Gear Coat for a Cheap Job	149
Gears for Business Wagons, To Paint	35, 36, 37
Gears, To Clean	140, 141
Gilding Machine	66
Gilding Size	64
Glazing	24, 25
Glazing Name Panels	37
Glazing with Carmine	49
Gold Bronze, Applying, to Wagons	67
Gold Leaf, Applying	64, 65, 66
Gold Paint	67
Gold Size	64
Gold Striping	64
Good Taste in Painting a Vehicle, An instance of	159
Ground Coat for a Business Wagon	34, 35
Ground Color for a Carriage	132
Hand, Position of in Striping	53
Colors (Harrison's Combination) in a Vehicle, An Example of	159
Harmony in Painting Vehicles Lost by Making the Bodies one Color and Carriage Part Another	158

	PAGE.
Harmony of Analogy, The	161
Harmony of Contrasts in Painting	161
Harness Leather, Use of in Hammering on a Painted Surface	147
Indicating by Colors the Difference in the Materials of Vehicles	158
Ivory Black, How to Thin	26
Last Coat on a Carriage	131, 132
Laying out Letters	96 to 103
Lead Color, How to Make	21
Lead Color, Method of Priming	28
Lead in Revarnishing Carriages	152
Lettering, Colors used for	108
Lettering for Wagons	70 to 110 inclusive
Lettering, Pencils for	107, 108
Lettering, Tools used in	107, 108
Letters, Abbot, Downing Co.'s Styles of	70
Letters, Balancing Properly	103
Letters, Boston Roman	89 to 95
Letters, Full Block	71, 72, 73
Letters, Full Block Octagon	72
Letters, Full Block Round	73
Letters, Gothic Half Block	98, 99, 100
Letters, Half Block	71 to 76
Letters, Half Block, How to Design	96, 97
Letters, Half Block Octagon	73, 74
Letters, Half Block Round	73, 74
Letters, Italic	77
Letters, Modern Old Style	80
Letters, New York Roman	81 to 89
Letters, New York Roman Italic	86 to 89
Letters, New York Roman Italic, Lower Case	88, 89
Letters, Ornamental	78
Letters, Outline	76
Letters, Printers' Black or German Text	77
Letters, Roman	80 to 95
Letters (Shaded), Various Styles of	108, 109, 110
Letters, Solid Block	77
Letters, Square Block	77
Letters, Tuscan Full Block	78
Lightening up a Job	63
Lines in Striping for Carriages	56, 57, 58
Materials, Care of	45
Monograms, English Style	167
Monogram, Florentine Style	167
Monogram, Louis XV. Style	170

	PAGE
Monogram, Modern Style	170
Monograms	165 to 170
Nickel Leaf	67
Oil, the Use of	20
Old Paint, the Uses of	148
Paint Brushes, Round	13
Paint, Cracking of	48
Paint, Crawling of	46, 47
Paint, Drying Qualities of, How to Test	19, 20
Paint for New Wheels (Carriage)	127
Paint for Repair Work, How to Mix	146
Paint for Second Coat on New Carriage Wheels	128, 129
Paint, Peeling off, How to Prevent	133
Painting a Body for a Cheap Job	149, 150, 151
Painting a Business Wagon Body	34, 35
Painting a Carriage Body	134, 135
Painting a Cheap Job	148 to 151
Painting a Spoke in Repair Work	146
Painting a White Job	69
Painting an Express Wagon	148 to 151
Painting Canvas Top Sides	48
Palettes, Zinc	53, 54
Panel Stripe for Spring Bars	58, 60
Painting Lumber Wagons	142, 143, 144
Painting Wooden Parts the Same as Iron, in American Carriages	157
Paints used for Lumber Wagons	142, 143
Pencils, Care of	54, 55
Pencils for Ornamental Striping	55
Pencils, Ox Hair	53
Pencils, Striping	52, 53
Pigments for Colors, Combination of	21 to 24
Pounce Bag, A	62
Priming	28, 29
Priming for a Cheap Job	148, 149
Priming Lumber-Wagon Boxes	143
Pumice-Stone Dust, How to Remove from Work	139
Pumice-Stone in Rubbing out	32
Putty	26, 27
Putty, Block	27
Putty, Block Bedding	27
Putty (Black) for Irons	27
Putty for Carriage Gears and Wheels	130, 131
Putty for Gears, How to Make	34
Putty Knife Method in Painting Business Wagons, The	38

INDEX.

	PAGE.
Putty, Quick	26
Putty, White	26
Puttying for a Cheap Job	149
Puttying Joints	139, 140
Repair Work, Touching up	145
Revarnishing a Carriage	152, 153, 154
Rough Stuff for Business Wagons	39, 40
Rough Stuff, Mixing	30, 31
Rough Stuff, Rubbing Out	32, 33
Rough Stuff, White	69
Rough Stuffing Panels	30, 31
Rubbing a Carriage	135, 136
Rubbing Down a Carriage for Revarnishing	152
Rubbing Out Rough Stuff	32, 33
Rubbing Process, The	37
Rubbing Stone, English	33
Rubbing Varnish	41, 42, 43
Rubbing Varnish, How to Apply	41, 42
Sand Papering a Carriage	131
Sash Tool, The	14
Schumachersche Fabrik	33
Scrolls (Flat) Designs for	118, 119, 120
Scrolling, Free Hand	111
Scrolling (Gold), Shading in	116
Scrolling, Harmony in	116, 117
Scrolling in Gold	115, 116
Scrolling, Leafing in	112 to 120
Scrolling, The First Lesson in	111, 112
Scrolling, The Line of Beauty	111, 112
Scrolling, Wagon	111 to 120
Scrolls, Flat	117 to 120
Shading	104 to 110
Shading Black Letters	106
Shading Gold Letters	105, 106
Shading Octagon Half Block Letters with a Double Shade Blocked	105
Shading Octagon Half Block Letters with a Single Shade Blocked	104
Shading, Position of Lines in	107
Shading Red Letters	106
Shop (The), And How it Should be Constructed	11, 12
Silver Bronze	67
Silver Leaf	67
Stencil, How to Make	121, 122
Stenciling	121, 122, 123
Stenciling, Brushes for	123

	PAGE.
Stenciling, Mixing Colors for	123
Stencils, Designs for	121, 122
Stripe for Back Ends of Shafts and Part of the Cross-Bar	61
Stripe for Top of a Spring	58, 60
Stripes for Wagon Gears	58 to 62
Striping Pencils	51, 52, 53
Striping, Straightening out	66
Striping Tools	51 to 55
Striping used on Business Wagon Gears	56
Striping Wagons	50 to 67
Touching up Repair Work	145, 146, 147
Transfer Ornaments	162, 163
Varnish, Blistering of	47
Varnish Brushes, How to Clean	44
Varnish Brushes, How to Keep in Good Condition	44
Varnish, Cracking of	48
Varnish, Crawling of	46, 47
Varnish, How to Mix for Carriages	133
Varnish Room, to Warm	41
Varnish, Specky	46
Varnish, Sweating of	43, 44
Varnish, The Finishing Coat of, for Carriages	134, 135
Varnish, To Lay On	42, 43
Varnishing	40 to 48
Varnishing a Carriage	133 to 136
Varnishing a Furniture Van	40, 41
Varnishing a Lumber Wagon	144
Varnishing a Sleigh	41, 42, 43
Varnishing a Wagon	41, 42, 43
Varnishing, Brushes for	133
Varnishing, Failures in	45, 46
Ventilator for Varnish Rooms	11, 12
Vermilion, Grinding	25
Vermilion, Light English	25
Vehicles, Angular Forms in	155, 156
Vehicles, Irregular Forms in	155, 156
Vehicles which Displease the Eye	156
Wagon, Business, To Paint	28 to 40
Wagons (Lumber), To Paint	142, 143, 144
Wagon Painting, Colors Required in	17, 18
Wagon Scrolling	111 to 120
Wood Filler for Priming, Wheeler's	39
Wood Filling on Business Wagons	39, 40

F. W. DEVOE & CO.,
Cor. Fulton and William Sts., New York,

MANUFACTURERS OF

DRY COLORS.

Colors in Oil, in Japan, and in Distemper.

VARNISHES AND JAPANS.

Pure Mixed Paint
FOR HOUSE PAINTING.

We wish to call your attention to the fact that we guarantee our ready-mixed paints to be made only of pure linseed oil and the most permanent pigments. They are not "Chemical," "Rubber," "Patent," or "Fireproof." We use no secret or patent method in manufacturing them, by which benzine and water are made to serve the purpose of pure linseed oil.

SAMPLES OF FIFTY DESIRABLE SHADES FOR CONSUMERS ON REQUEST.

MANUFACTURERS OF

FINE BRUSHES
OF EVERY DESCRIPTION,
AND ALL

Painters' Supplies, Artists' Materials, Etc.

COFFIN, DEVOE & CO., Chicago

SEND FOR OUR NINETY-SIX PAGE ILLUSTRATED PRICE-LIST OF BRUSHES.

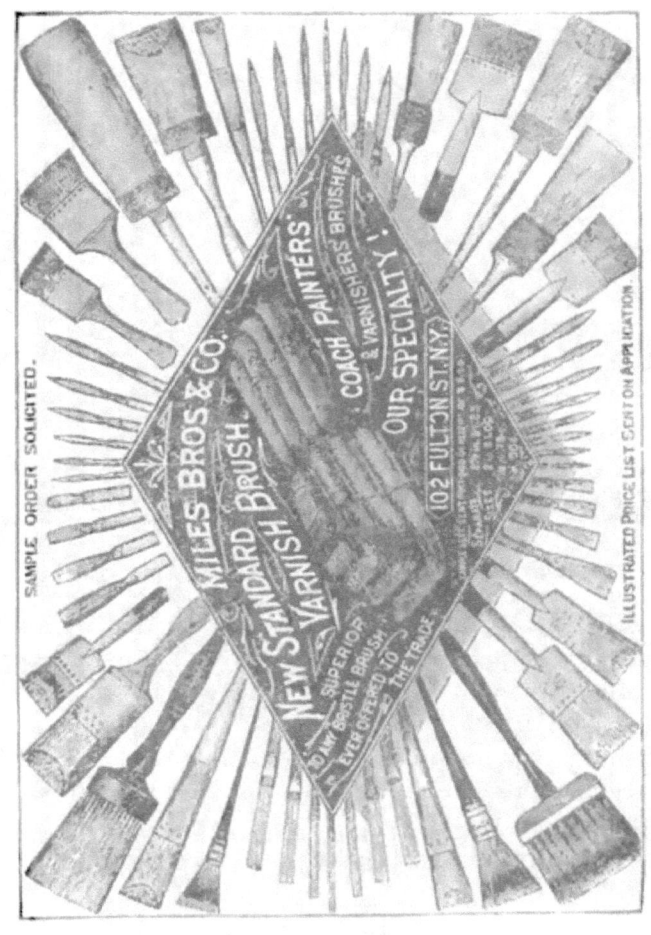

MILES BROTHERS & CO.,
103 FULTON STREET, NEW YORK

THE
Blacksmith and Wheelwright.

Every man who has anything to do with **BLACK SMITHING, CARRIAGE** or **WAGON BUILDING** or **HORSESHOEING**, ought to subscribe to this Journal.

It is distinct and different from anything else published.

Its **PRACTICAL ARTICLES**, many of them **ILLUSTRATED**, are worth many times the cost of a year's subcription to any mechanic.

TERMS OF SUBSCRIPTION.

One copy, one year, postpaid.....................$1.00
One copy, six months........ .... .50
Single number..... .... .10
Foreign subscriptions.... .... 1.25

ONE DOLLAR inclosed in a letter and mailed to us will entitle you, on its receipt, to THE BLACKSMITH AND WHEELWRIGHT FOR ONE DOLLAR.

A fraction over EIGHT CENTS A MONTH.

A trifle over TWO CENTS A WEEK.

It is not necessary to register your letter or procure a post office order, *but this course is recommended as being absolutely safe.* When not convenient to do either, send a postal note, or inclose the money in a letter carefully sealed, addressed and stamped.

Address all orders to

M. T. RICHARDSON CO., Publishers,

27 Park Place, New York.

P.S.—Specimen copies sent on application.

$1000 Worth of Law for $1.50

"How to be Your Own Lawyer" is the title of an entirely new book of over 500 pages, adapted for use in every State and Territory in the Union, and is by far the best and most complete work of the kind ever published. It gives instruction on all the most important law points which a Farmer, Mechanic, Merchant, or anybody else would want to know about, and if carefully studied and kept at hand for consultation when needed will save any man, in the course of an ordinary business career, hundreds, if not thousands of dollars. It is a lawyer whose retaining fee (the price of the book $1.50) has to be paid but once in a life-time. Plain and concise directions are given and forms furnished for the transaction of all kinds of business, and the preparation of every description of legal document in common use, such as Agreements, Bonds, Deeds, Leases, Notes, Mortgages, Wills, Etc. It takes up and treats in alphabetical order over 70 different subjects, as follows: Acknowledgment and Proof of Deeds, Administrators, Affidavits, Agents, Agreements, Apprentices, Arbitration, Assignments, Auctions, Bankruptcy, Bills of Sale, Bonds, Bills of Exchange, Cattle and Dog Laws, Collection of Debts, Common Carriers, Consideration, Contracts, Copyright, Corporate Associations, Custom House, Deeds, Divorce, Dower, Drafts, Executors, Exemption Laws, Farmers, Fences, Guaranty, Guardian and Ward, Highways, Hotels and Boarding-Houses, Husband and Wife, Insolvency, Insurance (Life, Fire, and Marine), Interest, Internal Revenue, Landlord and Tenant, Law of Place. Leases, Letters of Credit, Letter-Writing, Libel, Slander, Licenses, Lien Laws Limitation of Actions, Marriage, Master and Servant, Mining Laws, Minor, Mortgages, Naturalization, Pensions, Parent and Child, Parliamentary Rules, Partnership, Patents, Payment and Tender, Personal Property, Partition, Power of Attorney, Promissory Notes, Real Estate, Receipts and Releases, Rights of Married Women, Schools, Shipping, Subscription Papers (How to Draw), Trade-Marks, Trespass, Trusts and Trustees, Vessels, Voters, Wills, Warranty of Horses.

There is also a very complete Dictionary of Legal Terms; Tables for the Computation of Interest; Measurement of Land, Lumber, Logs, Grain; Legal Weight of a Bushel of Grain, Seed, and Roots; Quantity of Seed required to plant an Acre; Table showing Paper Required to make a Book of any Size; U. S. Land Measure; Number of Brick Required to Construct any building; Presidential Vote from 1824 to 1885; Time for holding Elections in different States; Population of the U. S.; Prices of various Commodities for fifty-three years; Valuable Rules for the use of Farmers and Mechanics; and much other important information. A copy of this valuable work, handsomely bound in extra cloth, with ink side-stamp, will be mailed to any address on receipt of $1.50. Address

M. T. RICHARDSON CO., Publishers,

27 PARK PLACE, NEW YORK.

www.ingramcontent.com/pod-product-compliance
Lightning Source LLC
Chambersburg PA
CBHW020251170426
43202CB00008B/323